D1589578

HUMANITY COMES OF AGE

HUMANITY COMES OF AGE

The New Context for Ministry with the Elderly

SUSANNE S.PAUL
and JAMES A.PAUL

BOOK SERIES

WCC Publications, Geneva

In addition to their own primary research, the authors have benefited in writing this book from published studies by many other researchers, as well as reports by United Nations and other international bodies. Because of the aim and format of the Risk Book Series, this book includes only a limited number of footnotes, documenting quotations and accounts drawn directly from earlier writers, and a select bibliography for the general reader of important titles on the subject of ageing. Those who wish to have a fuller list of books and articles may request one by writing to WCC Publications, P.O. Box 2100, 1211 Geneva 2, Switzerland.

Cover design: Stephen Raw

ISBN 2-8254-1048-9

© 1994 WCC Publications, World Council of Churches,
150 route de Ferney, 1211 Geneva 2, Switzerland

No. 64 in the Risk Book series

Printed in Switzerland

To our parents and grandparents
of our children:
Irvin, Lois, Jim and Jean
and to Oley, grandparent *honoris causa*

Table of Contents

Preface

"Ministry with Senior Citizens" was the theme of a consultation held at the Interface Academy in Pakenham, England, from 26 to 31 October 1991. Convened by the World Council of Churches' sub-unit on Renewal and Congregational Life, the consultation brought together 32 people, most of them from churches, academies and lay centres engaged in ministry with older people.

The consultation began with story-telling sessions, and visits to homes and hospices and centres and people involved in such ministry. Later there was a more systematic exploration of the issues that emerged from the sharing of information and the exposure experiences.

It was clear that the "ageing explosion" demanded of the church far more than what was being done through its ongoing programmes. It was also clear that in the countries of the South, the so-called developing countries, the revolution of long life was posing unprecedented challenges to families, churches and governments. The consultation brought out the crucial need for congregational education on attitudes towards and care of older citizens. Among the specific recommendations made by the meeting was the publication of a book that would contribute to increased congregational awareness on issues of ageing and the problems facing older people — including the basic question of how, and on what, they might live the rest of their lives.

Susanne, who was one of the participants at the consultation, was asked to write the book.

A few months later, as chairperson of the Non-governmental Organizations (NGO) Committee on Ageing at the United Nations, she was invited to attend the UN-sponsored assembly on ageing. The assembly, described as "a forum to launch an international action programme aimed at guaranteeing economic and social security to older persons", met in Vienna, Austria, in 1992.

When we began working on the book, we became more and more convinced that "old age" was not simply a demographic and biological fact; it was a socially constructed idea, loaded with emotional significance, and with political and economic implications. The project grew further as it also became clear that the issues of later life were not the object of benevolent intervention by governments and citizen groups worldwide, but rather the centre of a fierce debate over the distribution of resources and the future of human development.

We tried to understand why, in relatively well-off Hong Kong, many older people live in cages and rooftop shanty-towns; why governments have slashed pensions throughout Latin America; why the World Bank has pressed for health-care reforms that cut off services for older people; and why families everywhere assume less and less responsibility for older parents.

While considering these disturbing realities, we also discovered sources of hope — in the work and dedication of many ageing advocates worldwide (including faithful people in churches) and in the efforts of older people struggling for respect and rights.

The book tries to cover much ground in a short space. We have risked the danger of generalization in the search for themes that apply globally and can provide a basis for common action.

The book is built on the work of many others, to whom we offer grateful thanks. We hope it will answer its original mandate: to provoke reflection about policy and practice within the WCC constituency and to encourage congregational commitment to programmes with and for senior citizens.

SUSANNE S. PAUL
JAMES A. PAUL

Introduction

The revolution of long life is now upon us. In most countries of the world, until very recently, half of all human beings died before the age of twenty. Only a handful lived to see their grandchildren. But today, more and more people are living very long lives.

The long-life revolution comes as a victory in humanity's struggle against disease, starvation and violent death. But already alarmists warn that a world full of "old people" will be a world of contests over scarce resources. Who, they ask, will pay for the sustenance and health-care costs of these armies of elders? Who will take care of them? What good are they, anyway? Outrageous as these questions are, they define the callous indifference that is being urged upon us, in the name of "realism" or pressing economic "necessity".

While the ageing transition confronts the rich, industrialized countries with unexpected changes, it is proving far more difficult in the poor countries — the countries of the "South" — where more than three-quarters of the world's people live and where the population over 60 is growing fast. At a time of serious economic problems, long life is posing a tremendous challenge to human society. Governments, international agencies, churches, citizen groups and organizations of the elderly themselves are just beginning to address the tasks, including a radical rethinking of outmoded, unjust and deeply prejudiced conceptions of "old age".

Nearly everyone born today will have the experience of living in a different sort of society. People will have to assume more demanding responsibilities for older family members. Issues of income security and sustenance for older persons, as well as rising health-care costs, will loom ever larger on the political agenda. The conflict between demands that older people should work to support themselves and the situation of ever-declining job opportunities for older people may well reach the point of social explosion. Social policies, education, and economic activities of every kind will change. Churches and their ministries will have to change as well.

The future need not be a cruel struggle for limited resources as pessimists predict. Greater human dignity and social development are attainable in the years ahead, especially if all can contribute to the process. But that transition will not be easy or automatic. Great population shifts will require new approaches to employment, housing, health care, income support and social services. We need to consider how decent lives can be constructed with and for older persons under these new conditions, especially in the poorest countries where resources will be scarcest. Long life must be re-invented, to overcome illness, poverty, powerlessness, loneliness and isolation, to become an affirmation of human experience.

In rich, industrialized countries, long life is an established fact. For over a hundred years, governments have constructed social-welfare programmes for older people, including income security (pension) plans, health-care plans, special social services and the like. The great wealth of these societies made such programmes possible. But few are satisfied with the overall results. Mandatory retirement forces many healthy, vigorous people into idleness and boredom, as well as poverty and loneliness. Nursing homes and chronic care institutions often provide scandalously inadequate care.

Now, instead of renewing their commitment, governments of rich countries are turning away from programmes to improve the lives of their oldest citizens. Afflicted by economic troubles, governments have insisted on a harsh new social "realism" in the face of claims by older citizens for a better life. Many countries have pared back their pension schemes, health insurance and other supports for elder citizens, offering a horizon of *fewer resources*, not more, just when increasing numbers of citizens are pushed into early retirement.

In the poor countries of the South, transition to long lives proceeds much more swiftly and under far less promising circumstances. As governments grapple with international debts and domestic economic problems, resources for every social need are terribly scarce. In some regions, such as Africa and Latin America, poverty has grown dramatically, even though a few have grown very rich. No wonder, then, that many national leaders have ignored the special challenges that long life poses, content to affirm that in *their* societies and cultures, older people are effectively taken care of by families, friends or other local networks of solidarity.

The facts are different. Families and villages in the South are struggling under the impact of rapid economic change. Kin are migrating to distant cities or even across borders and oceans. Agriculture, where most elders have worked, is changing rapidly. Skills that were once useful are losing their value in an urbanizing world, while education and literacy are the province of the young. Elders find they no longer command respect as they did in the past. Families are breaking up. Millions of older people are now cast adrift in an emerging world which seems to have no place for them.

Some 300 million people over the age of 60 now live in the South and their numbers will double in the next thirty years. They have talents and energies, potential that can be applied to meeting basic human needs and to increasing social well-being. Their efforts can raise food and provide care for children and urgently-needed services of all kinds. What poor country can do without such a great pool of useful labour? But few poor countries today are addressing this issue.

In 1982, the United Nations convened in Vienna, Austria, a world assembly on ageing, drawing global attention for the first time to the policy issues of long life. Representatives of 134 nations at that meeting produced an international plan of action on ageing, which included many recommendations for improving housing, medical care, social security and other amenities for older people. The programme of the world assembly had been largely inspired by the European welfare state, with its government-sponsored retirement systems and other provisions. Its underlying assumption was: when people reach 60 or so, they should retire from work and receive support for the remainder of their lives. This framework, though well-meaning, has not provided a workable basis for global ageing policy.

In 1992 the United Nations celebrated the tenth anniversary of the Vienna gathering. By then, thinking had changed. There was far less enthusiasm for the "retirement model" and the idea that the later years of life should be marked by inactivity. In the new era, most agreed, no economy could bear such a burden, especially in the countries of the South. Further, even when affordable, the retirement model had never produced a satisfying framework. Instead of inactivity, the later years of life should involve productive activity, so that older people can remain socially engaged and contribute to their own sustenance and to the development of a good life for all.

The movement for "productive ageing" borrows from the actual practice of older people in simple rural villages. There, where pensions are unknown, people usually continue to work as their capacities permit. No artificial retirement age cuts them off from socially useful activities — or from the need to carry their share of the burden of subsistence. But how can this be recaptured in a radically-altered world economy, centred on cities and wage labour?

The "retirement model" increasingly has appeared flawed, because it thrusts people who have been active and independent into inactivity and dependency. It forces them to give up their sense of social purpose and dignity and to become dependent on the government, on the productive labour of others and on younger members of their own family. Even in the richest countries, most retired people suffer a major decrease in their income — so much so that a quarter or more of retired people are close to or below the poverty level.

To fill the void of income and social purpose, many effective grassroots programmes have been developed by citizen groups, including churches. Such programmes at their best are run locally, involve older people directly in decision-making roles, and empower the elderly to take control of their own lives. Some seek simply to ease the transition to retirement; others try to do away with the distinction, providing alternatives for active, productive lives. But as long as economic conditions include high unemployment, local initiatives to promote productive ageing will only have limited success.

Churches have traditionally done much work to care for frail elderly, work that goes back at least to the middle ages. They have built homes and hospices, developed home-care programmes, provided spiritual support, and given a focus of identity to millions of older people. But as the Pakenham conference made clear, churches have been slow to tackle the emerging issues of global long life. Church programmes have been far too paternalistic and too centred on ageing as an issue of frail persons in need of direct care. Building more institutional "homes" for the elderly will definitely not meet the needs of the new era. A completely new type of thinking is required.

Churches must join in the movement to affirm life throughout its lengthening course. This movement will keep older persons in the social mainstream, create new opportunities for socially-useful work, develop new sources of income, strengthen local networks of caring, build bridges among the generations and work for social solidarity at all levels. Churches must call for new approaches to employment that will ensure incomes and opportunities to all who want to work. Churches must help erase the stigma from age. They must call for national and (increasingly) global-level programmes that strengthen health care and develop other forms of support for long lives. Churches must reconsider the spiritual issues and priorities of the new conditions of long life. And, most importantly, they must encourage and empower older people to shape and build a style of life that suits them.

Acknowledgments

For their generous support of this project we would like to thank: the World Council of Churches; the Women's Division, the World Division and the Health & Welfare Ministries Program Department, General Board of Global Ministries, United Methodist Church; Church World Service & Witness Unit, National Council of the Churches of Christ in the USA; Global Action on Aging; and the United Nations Fund for Population Activities.

We would like to thank Tosh Arai and the participants at the Pakenham conference, where this book began. We would also like to thank the many people who have helped us on the project by sharing their own work, providing leads to other resources, commenting on the manuscript and generally providing a community of support and encouragement. We would especially mention Julia Alvarez, Elias Anzola, Evelyn Appiah, Maybelle Arolle, Ruth Bennett, Marcos Berezovsky, Alejandro Bonilla, Robert Butler, Bud and Millie Carroll, Elena Chalidy, Simone di Bagno, Colin Gillion, Jean-Pierre Gonnot, Alfred Grech, Akiko Hashimoto, Marcel Heisel, Ho Hei-wah, Irene and Delmar Hoskins, Helen Kerschner, Kevin Kinsella, Ji Seon Lee, Myrna Lewis, Elizabeth Mullen, Charlotte Nusberg, elmira Nzombe, Robert Palacios, Carolyn Peacock, Oglesby Paul, James Schulz, Nevin Scrimshaw, Tarek Shuman, James Sykes, Knight Steel, Ken Tout, Peter Townsend and Nadia Youssef, as well as Alexandre Sidorenko and the staff of the UN Ageing Unit. Special thanks go also to the members of the NGO Committee on Ageing at the UN, whose enthusiasm and dedication have been a constant inspiration.

We want to thank additionally the many people who agreed to be interviewed, those who helped with translations, and those who assisted us in the research process, especially the librarians at the New York Public Library.

We want to thank our sons, Timothy Schilling Paul and Jonathan Summers Paul, for their good-natured support of this project, and especially for Tim's extremely helpful editorial comments.

And finally we would like to thank our friends at WCC Publications.

1. The Transition to Long Life

Today we stand between two very different worlds, in a moment of dramatic transition.

Consider the era we are leaving behind. In terms of human survival it was no golden age. Many died in infancy or childhood. In tribal settlements, rural villages or squalid towns, people lacked adequate food and hygiene. Medical care as we know it was totally absent. Between a third and a half of all those born alive died before they reached their first year. Women often died during pregnancy and in childbirth. Floods, fires, earthquakes and drought wiped out large numbers. Famine, disease and war — often linked together — took their deadly toll.

In Europe, during the Black Death in 1387, nearly a third of all inhabitants died in the course of just two years — some 20 million people. In China, during the conquest of Genghis Khan, nearly 35 million (about a third of the population) are thought to have died of war, famine or pestilence in the decade after 1211.

In ordinary conditions of the 1600s in France, according to one estimate, a quarter of all people died before they were one year old; another quarter died before the age of 20; and yet another died before the age of 40. At about the same time, half the population of England died before the age of 20, and the average life lasted only 27 years.

Conditions favouring longer life appeared in Europe and America in the 1700s at the dawn of the industrial age. Public-health measures reduced disease, especially child mortality, and food and other life necessities became more plentiful. More children lived into adulthood, and more adults into advanced age, and average life-spans rose steadily.

By 1800 the average life-span in England had climbed from about 27 to 37. A century later, in 1900, it had risen to 48, and by 1990 it had reached 76. The United States followed an almost identical course. In just three centuries, the average life-span in both countries nearly trebled! These patterns are now being repeated, in far shorter periods of time, throughout the globe.

Already by 1950 — thanks largely to modern measures of public health and medicine and to more plentiful food — some 200 million people around the globe had reached 60 or more, a number greater than the entire human population of the planet during most of human history.

By 1990, forty years later, the revolution of long life had gained speed and spread to all the earth, dramatically altering the landscape of human society. The numbers of those 60 and over shot up to 500 million — more people than in all of Western Europe, twice the population of the United States, more than the population of Latin America. The numbers of those over 60 had started to climb by over one million each month.

By the year 2025, according to United Nations population specialists, the revolution will have gone much further: people of 60 and over will number an estimated 1.2 billion — 14 percent of the global population, more than the entire world population just 150 years ago. Their numbers will then be growing at 30 million or more per year.

The revolution of long life is most advanced in the rich industrialized countries. By 1990, in Sweden and seven other European countries, more than 20 percent of the population had reached 60 or over. Japan will soon have the longest-lived population of all. By 2020, the proportion of older people in these countries will have risen to one in three.

One demographer believes that by the year 2080, life-span in the United States will have reached 94 for men and 100 for women.[1] Some researchers talk of treatments that will extend lives still further. Even if extraordinarily long lives do not materialize, the global population will continue to live longer. Each year, fewer children and young adults will die. More people will certainly live on into their 80s and 90s.

Famine, war and natural disasters will continue to threaten lives, of course. And AIDS victims will probably grow in numbers in the short run. Surprising as it may seem, population experts believe that these tragedies will not substantially alter the trends towards longer life.

Longer lives can already be measured by the growing numbers who now live to 80 and over. Until recent decades some scientists even believed that this age represented a normal biological limit to life. But now everywhere the numbers who reach this age are rising swiftly. In 1950, just 13 million people worldwide lived to 80 or more. By 1990 the number had increased to over 50 million. And by 2025 it is estimated that nearly 137 million will have attained this age. As people learn to eat better, to keep fit and lead more active lives, an age of 80 will prove quite normal in the near future, even without dramatic and costly medical intervention.

Conditions leading to longer life have also transformed the pattern of human reproduction. All over the world, people are having fewer children and world population increase is slowing down. Eventually, probably sometime near the end of the next century, global population will stop growing and may even begin to shrink. With far fewer children, the proportion of older people will grow still faster.

For the first time in human history, parents can expect to see all their children live into adulthood — and children can expect to live into adulthood with both their parents living. Many parents now live long enough to know their children's children and perhaps even another generation as well.

Long life first appeared as a major social policy issue in Europe, where over a century ago governments started to develop programmes of retirement and health care for their citizens. Only in recent decades, as modern conditions have spread worldwide, has long life become an issue in the countries of the South, where the majority of the world's population live. Consider India. In 1901, the average life-span of its population was only 23 years; by 1961, it had doubled to 46; by 2020 it will have climbed to 68. The average life-span in China was only 29 in 1948. In the following thirty years, it grew to 63 — more than a year of additional life for each year that passed. By the year 2020, the Chinese will have a life-span of 75, with tens of millions of people in their 90s; and by 2035, nearly a quarter of the population will be over 60 years of age.

Some other countries began their ascent into the era of long life still more recently. Indonesia is one of the most dramatic cases, Jordan another. Even poor countries such as Lesotho, swept up in improved world health standards, have registered dramatic life-span gains.

Since 1975, the South's share of the global over-60 population has been growing rapidly, propelled especially by China, India and Indonesia. After the year 2020, countries such as Bangladesh, Brazil, Mexico and Nigeria will make the largest contributions to this shift. By 2025, an estimated 72 percent of the world's population over 60 will live in countries of the South.

Within the South there is a tremendous range of differences in the long-life transition. Some countries *already* have very high average life-spans. Hong Kong, Costa Rica and Jamaica are now ahead of the United States. And China, Korea and Uruguay are close behind. Cities in particular have long-lived populations. By 1980, more than one in five residents of Buenos Aires was over 60. At the other end of the range, some poor countries, such as Bangladesh and Mali, have life-spans barely more than half as long. But those that are furthest behind are moving ahead fastest. By the end of the twenty-first century, nearly every country will have arrived at long-life status.

Because countries of the South are passing through the population transition much faster than the industrialized first-comers, their shift to long life will have far more wrenching and unforeseen consequences. England had 250 years to adjust to its shift, while China's margin has shrunk to only seventy years. China's poverty, its forced-draft industrialization, and its radical economic changes will all complicate its long-life changes. Also, there is the sheer magnitude of the shift. In the thirty years between 1990 and 2020, China's population of 60 and over will increase from about 100 million to about 250 million.

In the same period, other major countries will experience even more rapid long-life transitions than China. By 2020, only a few countries in Africa which came late to the transition will not have high and rapidly-growing proportions of citizens in their 60s and beyond.

Poor and often lacking in decent housing, sufficient food and adequate medical care, the countries of the South will be hard-pressed to accommodate the radical changes that ageing has pressed upon them, especially at a time of austerity and economic difficulties.

What kind of life lies ahead for the new group of long-lived global citizens? The answer is not simple, for the lives of older people even in the industrialized countries are far from satisfactory. In these relatively prosperous lands, older people face poverty, age prejudice, depression, loneliness, abuse and the waste of their talents and labour. How much more problematic will the future be for those coming into advanced age in the world's poorest countries? The prospects for a decent life for over a billion older people worldwide remain the great challenge of the long-life revolution.

NOTE

[1] James Vaupel, as cited in Ricki L. Rusting, "Why Do We Age?", *Scientific American*, December 1992, p.141.

2. The Invention of "Old Age"

For thousands of years, poets and philosophers have reflected on the meaning of birth and death, youth and later life, but the concept of "old age" as a distinct and radically different stage of life is relatively recent. Beginning in Europe and North America, about the mid-1800s, "old age" came to be seen as a social "fact", marked by the same certainty and lack of ambiguity as birth and death. Once past the threshold of 60, "old" persons — regardless of their actual condition — came to be thought of as inefficient, unproductive, sick and even demented.[1] This newly-invented old age is now spreading rapidly to the countries of the South with dangerous consequences.

Until the nineteenth century, most people worked until they died, leading an active life through all their years. But industrial capitalism changed all that, especially with the high tide of factory production after 1850. Small farmers and agricultural workers, unable to make a living in the countryside, streamed into the cities, looking for wage work. But jobs were scarce and low-paid. Unemployment rose steadily. Social movements of the urban poor were a response to this situation, and they were often seen as a threat to the new social order.

Conservative social reformers like Bismarck and Disraeli looked for solutions to head off deeper change. Liberal reformers, too, backed by the more far-sighted manufacturers, searched for ways to moderate the emerging trade unions and socialist parties. Some promoted emigration to the colonies, others pressed for laws restricting child labour or protecting women from certain kinds of work. Most influential of all were Bismarck's sweeping new laws in Germany in the 1880s, founding disability and unemployment insurance and creating state-sponsored retirement. Each of these reforms rested on its own special logic, its own supposedly objective, scientific basis.

Women, for example, were seen as weak, emotional, undependable and best suited as home-makers. So, too, those over the age of 60 came to be defined as "old", decrepit and unfit for work. Experts, scientists, reformers, employers and clergy all played a part in this process of social redefinition. Ideas of social Darwinism, emphasizing the "survival of the fittest" and the biological determination of social life, gave credibility to the reforms. To them we still owe many of our ideas of childhood, disability, race, gender difference and old age.

In factories and offices, where previously people had worked until their 70s or more, employers began to lay off workers in their 40s or 50s. With no alternative means of livelihood, many older people could barely survive. By 1890, more than a quarter of all people over 65 in England had been reduced to destitution and pauperism. And in the USA by the late nineteenth century, old age was virtually synonymous with alms-houses for most of the population.

Reformers denounced the new conditions. Companies and governments — fearful of growing movements of political and social protest — introduced pension schemes. Government-sponsored social insurance, first set up in Germany in the 1880s and soon copied by many other countries, eased the pressures of survival for many older people. But by fixing a standard age and expectation for retirement, the reforms legitimized older employees' ejection from the work-force and helped define and fix the modern idea of a separate "old age".

The defining of old age

Most workers in the nineteenth century laboured for fifty or sixty hours a week, often under very bad conditions of health and safety. Many died in their 30s or 40s; those who survived were probably less fit by their 50s and 60s. As craft skills diminished in importance, employers preferred younger workers. An influential study by German engineer Ernest von Plener, based on a tour of British factories, concluded in 1871 that older factory workers were "worn out" and that younger replacements were more productive.[2]

Many other economists and engineers took up von Plener's themes in the decades that followed. German economist Lujo Brentano popularized the idea of unproductive old age in the years that social security was invented.[3] And during the following quarter century — as governments in many European countries introduced pension programmes — other authors in Germany, France, England, Holland and the United States developed theories about the economic deficiencies of older persons and their decline in value as workers. British reformer William Beveridge, for example, proposed the theory that older workers were more "inflexible". Other experts focused on how older persons had "used up their nervous force", or were "less energetic".

Employers hardly needed convincing. During the economic troubles of the 1880s, they pushed still more older workers out of the work-force and gradually introduced mandatory retirement based on age. Industrial efficiency studies convinced many employers of the "hidden costs" of older workers. By the turn of the century, many of the largest firms had introduced their own private pensions, especially where government pensions had not yet come into force. The Pennsylvania Railroad declared that its retirement programme ensured that its employees were "men at their greatest period of efficiency" and said that its modest pensions allowed the company "to get rid humanely of any drones who encumber the service to keep the entire staff constantly fresh".

As consensus built in favour of "retirement", some began to argue that national prosperity would benefit if older workers were systematically removed from the economy by government legislation. Laws mandating retirement appeared to complement laws forbidding child labour — seen as two steps forward in the march of progress.

In England and the United States at this time, medical and biological researchers laid increased emphasis on the "climacteric illness" which supposedly marked the transition from healthy maturity to the physical decline of "senescence". Grasping for explanations of a distinct old age, doctors spoke of "biological energy" as being exhausted and they claimed to find an "extraordinary decline of corporeal powers" in later life. Writing in 1884, one physician spoke of an "organic craving for rest", and in 1890, Charles Mercier spoke of ageing as the natural and inevitable result of the gradual subsiding of the molecular movement of the nervous elements into stillness.[4]

These notions of "rest" and "stillness" re-enforced the idea that retirement is biologically determined and they helped persuade a dubious public that withdrawal from work was both necessary and desirable once a certain chronological age had been reached.

Prof. William Osler of Johns Hopkins University in the United States — one of the pioneers of modern medicine and perhaps the most influential physician of his day — lectured about the "loss of mental elasticity which makes men over 40 so slow to receive new truths". He equated scientific progress with youth and fresh ideas. In a famous lecture in 1905, Osler spoke of the "comparative uselessness of people over 40 and the entire dispensability of people over 60".

Medical researchers in France took the lead in a movement which began to define advanced age as itself a disease. Autopsies of people who had died after especially long lives led physicians to conclude that irreversible pathologies had developed due to age alone, including such new discoveries as sclerosis of the arteries. "Ageing" took its place alongside other diseases like tuberculosis, with its own epidemiological studies, even though the "disease" could neither be transmitted nor cured, nor reliably diagnosed.

The disease model of ageing led to fantastic theories seeking to explain its origins. According to one respected theory of the early twentieth century, a major cause of senescence was "intestinal putrefaction".[5] The disease model also confirmed the separate status of this period in life. As one learned authority wrote, "old age" (beginning at 50) was one of the five "natural divisions in human development and decay".[6]

Physicians also concluded that long-lived people suffer from brain deterioration, and lapse inevitably into a mental disorder known as "senile dementia". In spite of ample evidence of mentally-fit persons of advanced age, the medical profession became convinced that dementia was a fixed condition of biological ageing. This mental decay was attributed to various physiological factors, including dying brain cells, starvation of brain tissue, "softening" of the brain, and so on.

One might imagine that with so much illness, medicine would have concentrated on old age, but just the opposite occurred. Most physicians argued that treatment of older patients was pointless. Treatment of the elderly came to be seen as the most unappealing and least prestigious area of medical science.

Doctors' treatment plans of the long-lived used strategies based on presumed frailty and general incapacity — even when treating robust patients. They urged older persons to avoid exercise, to rest and to prepare themselves for growing bouts of chronic sickness and infirmity. Books and tracts popularized these medical views and campaigners for social-security reform gave them further public notice when they emphasized the frailness of the elderly to win public support for their programmes. Ironically, then, just as the long-life revolution was producing large numbers of perfectly healthy people of advanced age, the ideology of decrepit ageing became firmly established. With the imprimatur of the scientific community, "ageing" came to be seen as a biological destiny, associated with decline and dysfunction of the body's major organic systems.

Churches, too, participated in the "invention" of the new forms of old age. In the late nineteenth century, sermons, devotional materials, hymns and prayers developed and spread the idea of a "weary" old age, close to death's door. Christianity provided its own special interpretations of the emerging life stage, considering it a time for distancing oneself from worldly concerns and preparation through prayer for death and salvation. New church publications such as the Methodist *Home Quarterly* and *Mature Years* reflected these views and provided devotional lessons for elderly "shut-ins".

Churches also began to think, as employers, about the issues of "old age". Like other employers of the day, they came to see their clergy and other employees as less effective in later life. Though John Wesley had led a vigorous life as preacher and religious reformer until his death at 88, his successors in Methodism questioned the value of ministers who had reached the age of 60. Church documents begin to speak of older clergy as "worn out" and needing or deserving a permanent "rest".

Churches adopted new or expanded pension programmes. Rules of mandatory retirement for clergy, missionaries and other church employees soon followed. Indeed, many churches placed age limits on lay persons' participation in governing bodies and other volunteer posts as well. As the rest of society, churches affirmed in their new practices a belief in the rapid and inevitable decline towards senility, senescence and death.

As a logical extension of such views, churches took the lead in founding new "homes" to care for the elderly, especially the elderly poor. Unlike the almshouses of earlier centuries, which gave shelter to older persons not presumed sick, these new homes were increasingly oriented to care for those considered prey to chronic illnesses. Care-givers, nurses and medical practitioners figured prominently in their programmes. Death, it was presumed, was just around the corner.

Churches built hundreds of such homes in cities and towns throughout Europe and North America in the nineteenth century and continued to build more in the twentieth century as well. These homes usually imposed a life of asceticism, prayer and celibacy, and frequently separated husband and wife. They stripped their inmates of any property and shut them up in a life of almost monastic detachment from the social mainstream.

Insisting that older persons withdraw from society and framing old age as a time for prayer and preparation for death, the churches sanctified age-based discrimination. And by defining pity and charity as the appropriate responses to the elderly, they re-enforced the movement which severed older persons from their accustomed life and labour and forced them into a state of indigent dependence.

Ageing, retirement and unemployment

Throughout the twentieth century, in the industrialized countries unemployment and "old age" have been woven ever more tightly together. In the face of a persistent lack of jobs, governments and employers have promoted retirement as a means of shifting and disguising unemployment. As a result, fewer and fewer workers over the official retirement age remain in the labour force. In 1890, 70 percent of men in England over 60 continued to work, but a hundred years later, only 20 percent remained in the labour force. Though some stopped working voluntarily, the overwhelming majority were forced to leave against their wishes.

The millions of people now classified as "retired", who really want to be working, should logically be considered as unemployed. If governments measured their unemployment rates on this basis, the results would show overall unemployment rates of 25-30 percent, a scandalous level. The retirement system, with its dole for the majority, escapes from potential political protest by a definitional sleight-of-hand.

Originally, many people opposed the retirement/"old age" system. Workers, trade unions and intellectuals at first spoke out against the implications of retirement. "Men shrink from voluntarily committing themselves to an act which simulates the forced inactivity of death," complained the *Saturday Review* in 1903.

But the fuss soon died down. Trade unions and reform-minded intellectuals came reluctantly to accept the logic of retirement, the "inefficiency" of older workers and the apparent inevitability of unemployment among older people. By the early decades of the twentieth century, there seemed little choice any more. Opposition dissolved. The welfare state and its assumptions seemed permanently established. Defence of pensions and even of the "right to retire" became a rallying cry of the left, not of the right.

Especially from the 1930s and 1940s onward, most people settled into a comfortable belief that "progressive" social reform would steadily improve the lot of the elderly, so that eventually everyone could look forward to a decent if not wholly pleasant old age. The level of public and private pensions rose, though slowly. Images re-enforced the idea of progress. Magazine photos showed former US auto-workers cheerfully playing bingo in Florida retirement communities and retired British railway clerks rocking contentedly by the Brighton seaside. But income statistics showed that poverty among the elderly remained widespread and that few really had the means to travel and enjoy what had come to be called the "golden years". And it was clear that mental-health problems were increasing. "There is no greater tragedy for the aged", said the US surgeon general in 1941, "than the unnecessary sense of uselessness which society now imposes upon them prematurely."[7]

Old age had increasingly become a social ghetto. Advertising and corporate culture constantly deepened the sense that "old" meant something bad or worn-out or pathetic. In a culture constantly reminded to "look young", with teenage models as the images of beauty, and youthful passion and action filling the cinema and television screen, elderly citizens could find little to affirm their role or culture. With lessened incomes and waning power and status, older people were commonly equated with outmoded fashion, outlived corporate priorities, obsolete equipment, discarded ideas.

Retirement and "old age" as a system required broad assent, even among the elderly themselves. Of course, a few dynamic and lucky individuals paid no heed to the new culture and carried on their lives as if time and age were of no importance. They were the exceptions that proved the rule. Most people, obligated to leave the workforce and assured that they had little left to offer, accepted unquestioningly the newly-invented reality and the assumption that human obsolescence was inevitable and even necessary. As time went on, retirement ages crept downward, even while progressivist optimism expanded.

Signs multiplied that something was amiss. Organized medicine neglected the treatment of the elderly, whose low income and social status made them less promising subjects for medical attention. Medical schools did not even teach courses highlighting treatment of persons in later life, and virtually all professionals considered facilities for chronic diseases of the elderly with contempt.

Conditions in old-age homes, revealed in one public scandal after another, proved equally shocking. And income for the great majority of the elderly remained pitifully low. A survey in York, England, in 1950 found two-thirds of the poor were people over 65.

Another wave of reformers zealously tackled the issue of "ageing" in the 1960s and 1970s. Hope again rose, as long-term care improved, pensions gained, medical coverage increased. The US Congress set up special committees on ageing and a national institute on ageing was formed. A variety of creative institutions like meals-on-wheels and home nursing care emerged in this period of ferment, to serve the frail and immobile elderly. An important group of reformers, led by Robert Butler, now began to call for "productive ageing", recognizing for the first time the broken link with the life of meaningful work.

But this new wave of reforms also failed to fulfill its promise. Culture remained "youth besotted" (as the *New York Times* later commented). Employers grew ever less enthusiastic about older workers. Half or more of older people reported that they felt lonely and useless. Material conditions for older people remained cause for concern as well: in the early 1990s, research found one in four elderly in the United States malnourished. And in virtually all industrialized countries older people suffered from widespread depression, inactivity and unnecessary physical decline. A survey in England showed that older people rarely left home and spent nearly forty hours a week watching television, and it noted that the "pensioner has that dire sense of withdrawal, of taking a back seat, of being the pit pony turned out to pasture for a brief, valedictory spell".[8]

As economies stagnated in the 1970s and beyond, corporate and government policies forced more and more citizens into early retirement. "Nearly every European

country has introduced some form of early pension programme," commented *Social Security Bulletin* in the late
1980s, noting that the purpose was "to readjust the labour
force... thereby creating job opportunities for younger
workers".

Corporate "restructuring" and "downsizing", moving
from Europe to North America in the 1990s, used early
retirement as a means of laying off millions of workers
with minimal political repercussions. As prejudice about
older workers among employers increased, actual evidence accumulated that older workers were equally if not
more "productive" than younger employees. A study of
the prestigious Commonwealth Fund in 1993 concluded:

> For most jobs, the productivity of older workers compares
> favourably with that of younger workers. A review of the
> literature indicates as many situations where productivity or
> job performance *increases* with age as where it decreases.
> Not only is age a poor indicator of performance, but
> researchers note that the average difference in performance
> across age groups is typically much less than the variation
> within each age group. Using age alone as a predictor of
> productivity is, quite simply, discrimination.[9]

The combination of long lives and ever-more-early
retirement strained the financial underpinnings of the
welfare state. By 1993 in Italy, the number of the retired
exceeded the number of active workers; everywhere,
fewer workers were supporting more retired people. With
far fewer children, the overall burden of "dependents"
actually had not changed, but governments took the
opportunity to trim their pension budgets and cut their
social-service outlays for older citizens. Led by conservative politicians like Reagan and Thatcher, a new kind of
harsh social Darwinism entered public policy discussions
— including strident demands for reducing (or even
eliminating) pensions and reducing (or age-restricting)
medical services.

"'Old age' can be viewed as 'living too long'," wrote retirement expert J.G. Turnbull with blunt candour, adding that old age means "outliving one's ability to secure an income through gainful employment."[10] Other experts began to warn that society would be ruined by armies of "greedy geezers" with their selfish special interests. Some even charged that old people were responsible for poverty among children. Blue ribbon reports and journals of opinion discussed the thesis that expensive programmes for the elderly were unfairly compromising the lives of future generations. The sages usually overlooked costs of military spending, regressive tax cuts, or forced worklessness of the elderly. "There will be generational conflict pitting American against American, child against parent, in a way that our nation has not seen before," warned the Concord Coalition. The Coalition and other organizations like it sought to undermine public support for old-age benefits and prepare the way for further cuts. In 1992, the US Senate eliminated its committee on ageing. Official neglect was becoming the order of the day.

At the level of daily life, the story was scarcely more encouraging. An advocacy organization wrote that older women were on *The Road to Poverty*.[11] Articles on mistreatment of the elderly filled the newspapers of the 1990s: abandonment by families, theft by kin and friends, abuse and even murder by those they depended on. A 1990s subway advertising campaign in New York City reminded citizens that taking money from the purse of an older family member without permission is the equivalent of stealing! Did previous generations require such moral advice?

At the same time, a growing number of "medical ethics" specialists proposed that governments deny older persons the right to expensive but life-saving medical procedures on the ground that medical costs were getting out of hand. Daniel Callahan pioneered this kind of thinking in 1987 in his book *Setting Limits*, where he spoke menacingly about a "natural life-span" and insisted that "America's elderly have no right to a creeping immortality at public expense".[12]

Predictably, respected authorities in the medical and scientific community joined the chorus. A well-known British biologist, Sir Peter Medawar, reprinted a notorious essay in which he complained about the "numerical tyranny of the greybeards". Dr Donald Gould, another scientific figure, published a similar article in the British magazine *New Scientist* in 1987. Using a sly, humorous style, Gould called for a "statutory limit on the right to life", backed by euthanasia. That such proposals are being made, in public or professional discussions, by distinguished scientists or cultural leaders, without storms of outrage, is a measure of how dangerous the social construct of "old age" has become and how seriously the "old age" group is at risk, even in the richest societies, with the longest public-welfare traditions.

How bad and how real is "old age"?

The literature on "ageing", whether by advocates or critics of welfare policies, shares one crucial element: it accepts "old age" as a social category and it accepts retirement as a natural arrangement. Advocates compound the confusion about "old age" with their own confusing mix of cheery optimism and puzzled pessimism and their spirited support for special status for the "elderly". In their urgency to propose new policies, such as special housing for the elderly, universities for the elderly, food programmes for the elderly, cheap movie and bus fares and all the other details of support for indigence in later life, they are often promoting age-segregation and supporting *sub rosa* the cause of a welfare or intellectual bureaucracy. They forget to ask why all this is necessary and whether it is the best way forward.

No one will deny that some people with unusual energy and life purpose are able to find very satisfying lives after their ordinary career is over — especially if they are rich or have large pension benefits. They may welcome the freedom from employment and be happy to embark on projects long deferred, and tasks they consider more important or more socially rewarding. Even those living in straitened circumstances may find fulfilment in caring for grandchildren, getting involved in religious work and social service, or letting a long-latent talent blossom. But by most accounts, the great majority of people in industrialized countries of the North do not have a successful "old age". A primary problem is that most lose half or more of their income and face a drastic reduction in their previous standard of living.

But the problem goes far deeper than the question of income. Older people face loneliness and the corrosive effects of age-prejudice. Being cut off from work lowers their self-esteem. Retired people also often say they lack purpose in their lives and feel unconnected to the rest of society. Many become passive, rarely leave the house, watch television much of the day, and sometimes fail even to attend to their own health and welfare.

To overcome the loneliness and purposelessness of "old age", governments and private organizations have produced networks of "senior centres" to bring human contact and interest into the lives of long-lived citizens. But such centres re-enforce the apartheid of the "old", and the activities that they promote are rarely a satisfying substitute for the active lives older people lived in the past. Special retirement communities, programmes and the like all contribute to the separation of the aged from the mainstream of life.

Looking at this combination of poverty and disconnectedness, researchers have come to describe life after retirement in grim terms. One well-known French expert has referred to retirement as "social death" and British historian Peter Laslett refers to retirement as it is usually lived as a "limbo" between life and death, the "end of worthwhile living".

Some have pointed out that the fears connected to being "old" begin to colour the outlook of people even before the age of retirement. By their late 40s, if not before, people begin to worry about their pension and how they will live in future without a job. In their 50s they may start to feel the pressure to leave their job and they may become concerned about disabilities, medical costs and the "burden" they might pose to their family. Death creeps up over the horizon. No wonder that the later years of life are such a subject of fear, and that being "old" is so deeply affected by taboos.

The "old-age" construct is rooted in supposedly objective scientific and medical judgments about physiology and human development. But, given the great variety in life expectancy from one country or population group to another, and the great diversity of the causes of death, long life as a physical process is not well-understood within the scientific community and it has continued to puzzle medical, biological and social researchers.

Government scientists, university specialists, and scientists employed by pharmaceutical companies and cosmetics firms have investigated the causes of infirmity in later life and ways to combat them. But so far, progress has been slim. No discovery has led to the lengthening of the life of those who live longest, and no clear theory of "senescence" or body decay has emerged. Science and medicine cannot confidently distinguish ageing as biology from ageing as a socially-determined process.

Biologists usually claim that, as life proceeds, human cells change their internal functions and lose some of their capacity. Studies have addressed the statistical likelihood and biological basis of deterioration in hearing and eyesight, changes in skin and muscle, reduction in bone mass, slowing of brain function and so on.[13] But none of these body changes — except the end of women's reproduction — happens predictably, at a given age or in a set range of years. Some people have keen hearing and eyesight until the day of their death, into their 80s, 90s and beyond. Some retain great powers of memory. Others have more stamina and strength at advanced age than those of younger people. In short, the infirmities associated with long life are only averages, not destiny, and they seem more closely connected to people's activity and environment than to their age.

Most importantly, as life-spans lengthen, averages for infirmities often shift upwards. In France, the number of people over 100 increased fifteen-fold from 1958 to 1992 and most of the recent centenarians rarely consult a doctor. Physical decline is very elusive, even to the medical and scientific professionals who study it. With science unsure of the meaning of "old age", and a century of "old age" social policy in doubt, it seems clear that ageing will have to be rethought, on a completely new social, economic and scientific basis.

Ageing crisis in the South

As rich, industrialized countries grapple with long life, deep difficulties emerge in the countries of the South. If the elderly in the North are now increasingly at risk in tottering welfare systems, the elderly in the countries of the South face far greater risks. Globalization of trade and investment brings radical change to the lives of billions of world citizens. In the South, "old age" emerges with a vengeance, even more explosively than it did in Europe and North America a century ago — not a welfare state version of old age, but a weak-state version, far harsher and more cruel.

Southern political leaders, to be sure, insist that their societies will never adopt the uncaring social arrangements of the North, that cultural "veneration" of the elderly and traditions of family solidarity will ensure a decent long life for all their citizens. But "old age" is being imported into the countries of the South as rapidly and ubiquitously as Coca-Cola.

As the old values of social solidarity dissolve in the global market-place, new values emerge which are no different from those of the North. Business managers from Hong Kong to Honduras are convinced of the advantages of young workers and refuse to employ older people, claiming they are "unsuitable", "unproductive", "uneducated" and "undynamic". "The work-place consistently discriminates against those over 35," concludes a report from Venezuela.[14]

A culture celebrating youth arises, linking old age with all that must be rejected about the past. New automobiles, new products, new cities, new values, these are the hallmarks of the age of developmentalism. Writers of various political persuasions, like Naguib Mahfouz of Egypt and Gabriel García Marquez of Colombia use elderly characters as symbols of corruption, decay, backwardness, ignorance.

NOTES

[1] For an historical analysis of views of old age, see Herbert C. Covey, "The Definitions of the Beginning of Old Age in History", *International Journal of Aging and Human Development*, vol. 35, no. 4, pp.325-37. Covey concludes that before the late nineteenth century the concept of "old" was flexible and related to a person's physical condition; with retirement the concept became much more chronological and defined in a new way.

[2] Cited in William Graebner, *A History of Retirement*, New Haven, Yale University Press, 1980, p.24.

[3] *Ibid.*, p.26.

[4] As quoted in Carole Haber, *Beyond Sixty-five: The Dilemma of Old Age in America's Past*, Cambridge University Press, 1983, p.74.

[5] Theory developed by E. Metchnikoff. See "Age", in *Encyclopaedia Britannica*, 11th ed., 1910, vol. 1, p.372.

[6] *Ibid.*

[7] As quoted by James E. Birren & Vivian Clayton, "History of Gerontology", in Diana S. Woodruff & James E. Birren, *Aging: Scientific Perspectives and Social Issues*, New York, 1975, p.23.

[8] *The British Gas Report on Attitudes to Ageing 1991*, London, British Gas, 1991, p.12.

[9] *The Untapped Resource*, New York, 1993, p.16.

[10] "Welfare and Social Security Programs", *Encyclopaedia Britannica*, vol. 19, Chicago, Britannica, 1983, p.746.

[11] Older Women's League, *The Road to Poverty: A Report on the Economic Status of Midlife and Old Women in America*, Washington, Older Women's League, 1988.

[12] New York, Simon and Schuster, 1987.

[13] Beverly Merz, "Why We Get Old", *Harvard Health Letter*, Oct. 1992, pp.9-12.

[14] Louise Margolies, "The Impact of Ageing Amid Sociocultural Change in Venezuela", in Ken Tout, ed., *Elderly Care: A World Perspective*, Andover, UK, Chapman and Hall, 1993, p.223.

3. Work and Long Life in the South

The old in rural areas

Amma lived in a village on the Volta River in Ghana. Until she died in 1963, well into her 80s, she raised crops of corn and peanuts, gathered firewood, cooked and cleaned, visited her neighbours, and participated in village gatherings. On the day she died, she came in from the fields, cooked dinner, bathed, got into bed and went to sleep, never to wake up.

Amma's productive, integrated ageing symbolizes the essence of long life until recent times. Before the coming of the market economy, work and activity in villages never stopped. "Retirement" did not exist. Long-lived people remained integral members of their community till the end. Old Kenyan women resolutely carried heavy loads of firewood, fodder and water. Old Moroccan men walked many miles with their goat and sheep herds.

Like Amma in Africa, Uncle Lagan on Angelis Island in the Bahamas worked hard all his long life. On the day he died, he walked seven miles round-trip from his house to his subsistence farm. After a full day of work in the hot sun, he came home, cooked his food, ate, lay down and went to sleep. According to his family he was 103 years old.

In Kombone province of Cameroon, nearly all men over 60 are still active in work outside the home and about two-thirds of the women of the same age work as well. Most of the others do household tasks, tend animals and produce handicrafts. Virtually none depends completely on the community for support and sustenance. Elise Bakang, the wife of the chief in Mahomy village, worked in the fields nearly every day raising yams, yucca and peanuts from dawn to dusk into her 80s even though she had borne and raised twelve children.

Grandma Migdim, of the Awlad `Ali Bedouin in Western Egypt, set an impressive pace as matriarch of one large family and a senior member of another. Though bent nearly double and walking only with the help of a stick, she presided at weddings, funerals and feasts as well as sickbeds. At home she was always busy — spinning, winding yarn, sewing burlap sacks to patch the tent, tending the goats.

Even elderly of wealth and social standing continue to work as an affirmation of their power and dignity. Ahmad, the patriarch of a large Lebanese family in a village in the Bekaa Valley, worked every day until just before his death at 85 a few years ago. In the summer he rose at dawn and worked in the fields with his sons, tending corn, potatoes and tomatoes, and running the affairs of his numerous clan.

Atorjan, a prosperous widow in rural Bangladesh who lives with her son, is similarly active. She cooks, washes, sweeps, makes rope, dries and sells the family's rice, picks food from the garden, and takes care of the cooking utensils. Poorer women, hired by her son, do the heavier work connected with harvesting the rice crops. [1]

Work in traditional village society was always woven into the fabric of all life. Older people, who often lived with their offspring, usually had special tasks, often based on gender. The oldest woman commonly assumed responsibility for taking care of the children, made clothing, wove baskets and was busy with other domestic tasks as well. The oldest man settled disputes, told stories, organized festivals and led in the planting and harvest. Typically, the elderly commanded special honour and respect for their wisdom, experience and links to ancestors.

Today, the majority of long-lived people in countries of the South still live in simple agricultural villages, especially in Africa and Asia. Millions still work as they used to, in traditional agriculture. The poorest countries, where subsistence agriculture persists, witness the largest proportion of elderly workers.

Recently in Malawi, 85 percent of all men over 65 were counted "in the labour force", in Liberia 70 percent and in Guatemala 63 percent. Such statistics probably underestimate the real number of older workers in these poor lands. Women tend especially to be undercounted, but they work at least as much as — or more than — the men.

Still, village life has changed drastically over the past few decades, sweeping away many conditions that gave security and stability to the lives of older people. Many villagers today no longer have free use of a plot of land, or their plot is too small or arid to support them. Growing population, deteriorating environment and specialized agriculture that favours big farmers — these are some of the factors that deprive families of adequate land. Instead of subsistence farming, people must now work for wages, often on a large farm or plantation, raising cash crops like tea or jute, or sugar cane or pineapples. In Bangladesh, half of all rural families are landless — up from one in five just thirty years ago.

In this changing rural scene, old people have far less opportunity to live a productive life. With the spread of the market economy, as dependence on wage work grows, they increasingly lose their grip on opportunities for productive labour and they often cannot support themselves. From the rice and sugar plantations of Brazil to the tea estates of Sri Lanka, employers say they prefer the greater strength and "adaptability" of younger workers. "When you leave off producing, you lie around till you die," said one unemployed older worker in Brazil.

Large agricultural companies now often shift crops and investments, dumping older workers into sudden unemployment. In Trinidad, the sugar companies are closing down their old plantations as they move into highly-mechanized rice, cocoa and other crops. Older cane workers in places like Papano Village have no chance of work, and no income on which to live.

In Kerala state in India, sweeping land-reform programmes virtually eliminated tenant-farming. Earlier, landlords used to assume a certain responsibility for old people; they would offer continued work, provide some health care and housing. Today, this is no longer the case.

Even in China, where most people in the countryside could be assured of work until recently, elder unemployment and destitution have been growing. Ageing Zang Hongbin and his wife Liu Xiaoying, who live in a leaky little hut with a mud roof in a rural village, eke out a living recycling garbage.

In many countries, the change to worklessness has come with brutal swiftness. Two-thirds of older Turkish men were counted as workers in 1975, but just thirteen years later only one-third of men over 65 still had gainful work. In Costa Rica the proportion dropped nearly as fast. Women lose work opportunities, too; it is often said that employers prefer girls and young women, and not always because they are more efficient. Women find it extremely difficult to find wage work after the age of 40.

Conservative writers sometimes argue that the elderly withdraw from work out of choice — that they are "tired" and prefer leisure. Some like to claim that the elderly have "earned their rest". Few elderly would agree. Without alternative sources of income or meaningful life, they are not satisfied with the poverty and aimlessness which unemployment imposes on them.

A survey in South Korea found that unemployed older people have a strong desire to work — mainly for income but also to overcome loneliness and to satisfy other social needs. More than seven out of ten people in their 60s want to work, and nearly a third in their 80s want employment as well. Prof. Yoon-Suk Lee, an expert on elderly health, concludes that "the elderly find value in their lives through their contribution to society". The same urge for work, income and social connectedness drives the lives of the elderly in virtually every country of the South. "Given the opportunity, most older persons would prefer to work," concludes a report from Singapore.

Faced with destitution, many older people take up casual labour, like selling trinkets in local markets or working as porters or watchmen. Still, they may not earn enough to feed themselves. Some scrounge for materials from local construction sites, while others search for discarded food. Some take up begging. Others, weakened and depressed, simply waste away and die from malnutrition.

Most older persons in the countryside now live in desperate poverty — in nearly every world region and country. Surprising numbers are in debt and even in debt-bonded servitude. In Indonesia more than a third of those over 60 are among the poorest of the poor, a proportion which rises to over half in rural areas. In Argentina, more than two-thirds of those over 65 in the countryside are living below the poverty line. In Belize three-quarters of the rural elderly are in extreme poverty and many have no job or visible means of support. And in Loma de Cabrera, a rural district of the Dominican Republic, nine out of ten older people in 1990 said they did not have enough to live on and nearly a third were almost totally destitute. Worldwide, an alarmingly high proportion of the rural elderly — perhaps as many as a third — live below the minimum level of subsistence.[2]

According to some reports, many older people, overwhelmed by life's problems, stop eating even when food is available. In India, for example, many are said to view self-starvation as a dignified, admirable way to end one's life, especially for a widow. But most often, elders stop eating because they no longer have access to food. Village elders are ready to die because they no longer feel they have much to live for. Maybelle Arolle, a missionary doctor in India, told us:

> In years past, they felt they had a definite role in society through raising food and helping to bring up the children. But now their role has collapsed and they feel they are not wanted any more. Many just give up.

Elderly in cities

When all city dwellers feel pressure for survival, old people face special disadvantages. They are less likely than younger people to be able to get or hold a job in conditions of vast and growing unemployment. Southern employers, like their counterparts in industrialized countries of the North, have come to prefer younger workers, who are believed to have more up-to-date skills, be less "worn out", or have some other perceived advantage. Most booming Asian electronics firms hire workers in their teens and discharge them before they reach 30; most workers in the roaring factories of Mexico's *maquiladoras* are between 15 and 25. Early industries in the North followed the same strategy: employing young workers and quickly using them up physically through hard work, long hours and dreadful conditions.

In Singapore, the government proposed raising the retirement age from 55 to 60 in 1988, but private companies resisted so strongly that officials backed down. Nearly half the companies in one survey said that older people "cost too much" and that they had "lower productivity". The same narrow criteria of efficiency and prejudices against older people that emerged in the West a century ago have begun to take root in the South today.

Trade unions, too, like their counterparts in the industrialized countries, have often pushed employers and governments to retire older workers so as to "make room" for unemployed younger people. From Costa Rica to India, strong trade-union movements have accelerated the exclusion of older people from the labour force, though they have often insisted on pensions and other state programmes to support workers in their later life.

But, of course, only a few have pensions. The rest often live on the margins of survival. A 1975 study by the Chilean national employment service concluded that "the aged population confront a very unfavourable economic situation, infinitely worse than the overall population". Half the population over 60 in greater Santiago were found to be living on half the minimum adequate per capita income or even less.

Some governments have callously promoted retirement of older wage workers as a means of generating employment for the young — exactly as in the countries of the North. Ironically, China — well-known for its elderly leaders — began an active campaign of this type in 1979, "designed to move older people out of the work-force as fast as possible" in order to open up jobs for an estimated 10-20 million unemployed urban youth. By raising pensions and allowing jobs to be passed on to adult children, the Chinese government hoped to push large numbers of workers aged 55 and over out of their jobs. The government even tried to get rid of the elderly from the cities by offering bonus payments designed to get people to retire in rural areas. Since 1986, China has strictly enforced its mandatory retirement system and increased its incentives for early retirement. Jamaica has faced the same dilemma. With unemployment so high among the young, asked its report to the World Assembly on Ageing in 1982, how could the government provide jobs for the elderly as well?

By comparison with regular wage work, with all its uncertainties, small businesses offer some hope of regular income and continuity of labour into advanced age. Evelyn Mitchell moved to Liberia's capital, Monrovia, in her 50s and opened a rice store in front of her house. The flourishing business helped support a large family and many grandchildren into her 60s and 70s.

But only a few are lucky enough to have such a regular business. Far more must work in the informal sector, which offers a nightmare of insecurity and low income. In 1990, casual labour accounted for half of all the urban work-force in Asia and Latin America and an astonishing two-thirds in sub-Saharan Africa.

Nearly all working urban elderly depend on the informal sector for survival. Some continue to work as household servants, but most crowd the urban market-places, selling vegetables, eggs or chewing gum, often sitting on the ground, without even a stall, liable to be stepped on, harassed by police, overcome by the heat or cold. Sometimes, elderly vendors come to monopolize a particular product — in China, older women are traditionally ice-cream vendors. Elders also often sell simple home-made goods, like knitwear, wood carvings, or — most often — cheap food. But whatever they sell, and however hard they work, they rarely earn a decent livelihood. As rents and other costs in the cities rise, millions of old people face destitution. Like their rural counterparts, the urban elderly may be forced to turn to begging. At a conference on ageing in Latin America held in June 1986 many participants mentioned the sharp increase of elderly beggars on city streets.

The lot of older women is still worse. In subsistence villages, women continue to work in agriculture and in family care until their death. But as market relations spread, women lose their connection to work — even more completely than men, and especially in old age. Urban patriarchal cultures often exclude women of all ages from work outside the home. In the Middle East and Africa in particular, women rarely work in factories, government service or other kinds of wage labour. Throughout the South, women's participation in the formal economy is far below that of men. Women work hard, but they work without wages within the household or in family agriculture. As such, they are considered "economically inactive", no matter how hard they may work. Women are handicapped by less education and less training in job-related skills. Even in the informal sector, they participate less than men in many countries. And as they age, they "work" outside the home less and less. In Guatemala, 72 percent of men over 60 are counted as employed, but only 16 percent of women.[3]

Since women live longer than men — from about a year longer in India to nearly seven years in Uruguay — they face a much greater challenge of subsistence in old age. The crisis of worklessness and unproductive ageing is most acutely a woman's problem. Old women scrounging in garbage cans, sleeping in doorways, begging pitifully at the entrance of railway stations, symbolize this growing scandal of discarded lives and doubled gender-risk for older women.

Adverse effects of structural adjustment

During the economic troubles of the 1980s, conditions of the elderly worsened in both countryside and the cities. Many countries of the South saw the prices of their products fall on world markets. Debts to banks in the North rose alarmingly. And growing unemployment led governments to focus attention on jobs for youth and young adults and to play down the importance of the elderly.

Economic conditions for the old have deteriorated further, as the International Monetary Fund, the World Bank and other agencies have put pressure on countries of the South to reduce the government's role in the economy, privatize state companies, eliminate price subsidies, reduce social programmes and slash government payrolls. To enforce such reforms, the Bank and Fund have imposed "structural adjustment programmes" (sometimes appropriately known as "shocks") on over ninety countries around the world. Structural adjustment offers new loans to cash-hungry governments if they agree to carry out these draconian reforms.

Under structural adjustment, unemployment and poverty grew rapidly, as the UN Children's Fund, the World Health Organization (WHO) and the International Labour Organization (ILO) have all shown in their studies.[4] The World Bank proclaimed its primary goal was "poverty reduction" but the real results were just the opposite.

In light of all this, many in Latin America and Africa refer to the 1980s as the "lost decade", a period when their economies actually declined steadily in per capita terms. "In most countries, the reforms have yet to lead to improved economic performance," concludes the UN Development Programme, in a tone of polite understatement. The Bank has conceded that among ninety countries worldwide it put through the wringer, nearly half suffered from a decline in per capita income during the entire decade of the 1980s.[5]

Nearly everywhere, old people suffered disproportionately. Extremely vulnerable to economic downturns, they lost opportunities for employment and productive work. They lost through much higher prices of necessities — the equivalent of a 15-25 percent drop in their real income, according to Colin Gillion of the ILO.

The elderly also lost the support of other government aid programmes that previously provided them with a vital margin for survival — programmes of work, health, family aid and the like. Governments and international lenders made no serious effort to shelter the elderly from these blows. The private-sector emphasis of the 1980s and '90s led to greater income inequality and still greater insistence on "efficiency". As the reform process continues, older people in countries of the South face further declines, with little hope of immediate improvement.

Work opportunities for the elderly

Governments of the South have done little to improve work opportunities for older people. Their typical development projects have been large-scale dams, electricity stations and steel mills, promoted by foreign lenders like USAID and the World Bank. Governments have tended to ignore small-scale, locally-based development efforts that could help long-lived persons, and they have usually assigned a low priority to development in rural areas, where the majority of the elderly live. But as the elderly increase in numbers, governments and foreign aid agencies may be forced to rethink their priorities and development strategies. Labour must be at the centre of all programmes to assure income and well-being to older citizens.

Botswana has developed a labour-based relief programme in response to the terrible effects of a long drought. In 1985-86, some 70,000 people of all ages worked on building roads, airstrips, small dams, latrines, community gardens, etc. Under World Bank programmes, some countries — including China — have also introduced food-for-work schemes in the poorest areas. China's programmes focus on building or improving agricultural terracing to increase local food production. Even when projects like this do not directly target the elderly, they tend to improve conditions for most older people by raising family and community living standards.

Other governments — including India and the Philippines — give funds to locally-based organizations so that they can hire elderly people for public-welfare projects. As early as the 1960s, the Philippines government set up a self-employment assistance programme, which gives small loans directly to older persons to start their own business.

In South Korea, the government set up several employment-promotion schemes for older workers beginning in the 1980s. One South Korean programme, begun in 1981, provides a special job referral service ("job bank") for older citizens, based in the Korean Senior Citizens' Association. Another programme, started in 1986, employs the elderly in workshops, making garments and other light manufactured goods. And a third programme established in 1991 gives priority to elderly persons to set up concession stands in parks and other public places. Such initiatives are helpful, but in fact they produce only a small fraction of the employment that would be needed to absorb all the energy and talent of the Korean aged.

An experimental centre for the aged, sponsored by the city of Rosario in Argentina, tries to find work for older people in far harsher economic conditions than those in Korea. It trains people in skills that are in short supply, keeps in close touch with local employers, and runs a labour exchange. Through ties to many senior centres and other institutions throughout the city, and through programmes to raise food and produce handicrafts, the centre has enabled many older people to survive in very difficult economic conditions.

Government-sponsored cooperative movements have provided work for older citizens in a number of countries. Governments provide credit and marketing to farmers and other producers, helping the elderly both directly and indirectly through these broad rural support programmes. In India, a movement of over 5 million farm families in 49,000 village cooperatives produce milk, much of which they sell and some they keep for their own consumption. Such cooperatives more targetted towards the elderly could help engage older people again in productive activity. The Committee for the Promotion and Advancement of Cooperatives (COPAC) has proposed greatly widened use of consumer and producer cooperatives by the elderly, arguing that coops are especially well-suited to small-scale elderly self-help projects in countries of the South. COPAC refers to successes in a range of different coops, including cooperative welfare centres in India and even a coop for funerals in Bogota, Colombia.

In the Dominican Republic and in several countries around the world, the British-based Save the Children Fund has launched projects which generate jobs for old people in child care or early childhood education, usually with government funding. By the late 1980s, UNESCO and other UN bodies expressed a growing interest in this initiative. In March 1989, following a UNESCO request, a European research institute produced a major report reviewing global progress. UNESCO followed up with a meeting of experts in November of the same year in Wuhan, China. These initiatives are often closely tied to programmes for further education of the elderly.

Though experts and elderly participants are enthusiastic, governments have not moved very far with this approach. Most continue to favour hiring younger and better-educated staff. Education ministries feel it is not their responsibility to deal with problems of the elderly. When polled by UNESCO researchers, many governments admitted that they lacked a policy for support of their elderly citizens and most fell back on formulas about the need to strengthen the family.

Overall, in the 1980s, governments did less than in the previous decade to help their older citizens. Also during the same period, large international aid and development agencies remained inert on the issue; most often, they did not have programmes or even official positions on the elderly. Ageing advocate Julia de Alvarez reports that when she asked the Dominican administrator of the United Nations Development Programme what his organization was doing in the field of ageing, he replied "nothing", and looked at her as if she were "a little eccentric for even raising the issue".[6] The World Bank did not have a policy statement on ageing until well into the 1990s and it has no special office or programme focus on the development role of the elderly.

In this vacuum, churches and a few pioneering private citizen organizations have taken most of the initiative. In addition to traditional programmes of charity and emergency aid — such as handouts of food, clothing or other necessities — they began to experiment with work-generating projects. They set up workshops for light manufactures such as clothing and crafts. The Human Development Centre, a Catholic agency in Bangkok, established a successful workshop of this kind for destitute old people in the Klong Toey slum. Cebu Caritas in the Philippines teaches low-income elderly traditional crafts like bamboo work and basket-making as well as more modern skills such as the use of a sewing machine and even television repair, as part of a work-generating programme. In Hong Kong, a private group set up a placement project which does more than simply find jobs: it encourages the elderly to work and employers to hire them. But the most innovative programmes are considered to be small, locally-based business enterprises, generating "self-help" income for even the poorest elderly.

Small businesses have been run for many years by the elderly on their own initiative. Older women in Ghana have been active as merchants and wholesalers, especially of food. Some have established and run the famous "mamabanks" — informal saving and lending institutions which help other women traders.

The London-based Help the Aged pioneered in promoting self-help in the 1970s, becoming the first organization focusing on development and ageing. Its founders broke away from the social-security model of retirement, understanding the vital importance of employment and income to the elderly in poor countries. They set out to create the needed employment by means of small enterprises. Affiliates were soon set up in India, Kenya and other countries, and a network called HelpAge International came into being in the early 1980s.

In the 1970s and '80s, as micro development projects came more into fashion, a number of churches and other private organizations started what some call "senior enterprises". Today there are thousands of elderly self-help projects all over the world, with 26 HelpAge affiliates in developing countries. HelpAge International's budget — at slightly over $1 million — is large in the international ageing field, but minuscule in comparison with need or with spending for other purposes. The World Bank's lending in the same period was 19,000 times larger.

HelpAge and other agencies usually invite project ideas from locally-based groups. Support takes the form of a start-up loan and technical advice for planning and management. One such project helped local fishermen build their own boats, another helped people set up a local bakery, yet another provided seedlings to start a local nursery. Some projects have succeeded beyond all expectations and have generated work for dozens of people. A kerosene distribution coop in Kenya generated a profit equal to its initial investment in just fourteen months, while meeting a real community need. Other projects have promoted recycling, produced inexpensive herbal medicines for local use and revived beautiful handicraft skills.

May Belle Arolle, a Methodist doctor who has been serving the poor in Jamked district in India for more than twenty years, has helped set up such projects. According to Arolle, the people ensure that the plans fit local needs and expectations. A goat-rearing programme allows poor old people to start a small personal herd; with five or six animals they can comfortably support themselves. A tree-planting project in the same area supports soil conservation and yields fruit crops which elderly people can take to market. Women run most of the projects. By providing work and encouraging self-sufficiency, these projects give old people both income and social dignity. They have had a transformative effect in the area of Jamked, known for its deep poverty.

Caritas, a Catholic charity, supported a project for older people in the town of Chacon in Chile to breed angora rabbits and practise organic gardening. Caritas provided rabbits and seeds, as well as technical assistance, and the recipients repaid the "loan" in kind. Some two hundred elderly now participate; they shear the wool from the rabbits, spin it and dye it. They can earn a relatively good income with only minimal access to land or other resources. Caritas hopes to have several thousand people eventually involved.

Indigenous movements emphasizing self-help include the Sarvodaya Shramadana movement in Sri Lanka and the Groupements Naam in Burkina Faso. Though they do not direct their work at the elderly, they have set up successful income-generating programmes in thousands of villages which have directly or indirectly helped older residents.

A few special institutions like Bangladesh's Grameen Bank are making commercial-type loans to the self-help sector. The Grameen initiative started informally in 1976 when development economist Muhammad Yunus realized it was impossible for landless villagers to get loans from existing commercial banks. He started to guarantee loans himself in one village where he was working and found the repayment rate to be very high. In 1983, he founded the Grameen Bank, with funds from the Central Bank of Bangladesh and various foreign donors. By 1991 it had established nine hundred branches serving 23,000 villages and had offered credit — on average $60 — to a million households.

Grameen is able to lend without any collateral and at relatively low rates of interest, because repayment is guaranteed by a group of five people in the local community, including the person taking out the loan. The bank has been so successful that many other countries have sought to copy it, including Bolivia, Guinea, Indonesia, Peru, Mali and Pakistan. Indonesia's two institutions, the Kupedes and the Badan Kredit Kecamatan have together made over four million loans. This semi-commercial lending promises to increase dramatically the pool of funds available to self-help projects, enabling them to reach far larger numbers of people. At present, though, the scale globally still remains small compared to other development initiatives. Further, unlike HelpAge, Grameen's lending does not target or privilege the elderly.

Problems with self-help

Many advocates of the elderly worry that private self-help may create false impressions: it may lead people to believe that private initiatives for the elderly are sufficient, and that government programmes are not really needed. They point out that governments have been trying to shift attention to the private programmes, so that they can cut their own funding without facing public protest. But private citizen organizations cannot succeed without active government partnership. According to Joan French, a Caribbean advocate of the elderly:

> The fact that the state is abandoning responsibility for people is affecting not only NGOs but those government departments and agencies to which NGOs and people in need could look for support in the past... In this situation, the state often tries more and more to court NGOs, to get them to take on the responsibilities that the state has abandoned. Never have NGOs been more in vogue...

Critics argue that many private organizations remain silent, fearful of antagonizing governments in countries where they work, instead of defending the cause of the elderly against government cutbacks. Silence can be a form of complicity with the governments and a refusal to press for the conditions that are essential if self-help is really to succeed. Feeling the squeeze in their own budgets, nearly every large international organization has opted for caution instead of courage.

Self-help projects themselves suffer because they often have too many competing goals. A bakery in Bogota, Colombia, set up by the Catholic organization Pro Vita with international support, pursued three goals: to provide work for elders, provide free or low-cost bread to old people's institutions and generate a profit to support a clinic for the elderly. Not surprisingly, it ran into difficulty. It couldn't even balance its budget because it was giving too much of its bread away free![7]

Other projects run into trouble because they confuse production for need with production for the market. Some other projects, including laundromats, bakeries, poultry and rabbit farms, and handicraft establishments have found that not only are neighbours often too poor to buy their products, but that success may lead large competitors to move in and challenge their place. Successful self-help projects sometimes must sell their goods to tourist hotels or other well-heeled clients; they are unable consistently to produce for the direct benefit of their community.

Self-help projects can also raise the ire of businesses or money-lenders who want to maintain their own lucrative positions in the local economy. When HelpAge aided fishermen in a village in India with logs to build new boats after a typhoon, the plan cut out businessmen who previously charged exorbitant rents for the boats and kept a marketing monopoly on the fish. The plan provided a better income for the fishermen and for the village elderly.

But the businessmen were furious at losing their profits on the indigent villagers' servitude. They tried to stop the project with what has been described as "unpleasant" forms of intimidation. If an international organization and the central government had not been involved, the project would apparently never have succeeded.

In spite of all the financial and technical support, self-help projects have a relatively high rate of failure, like small businesses everywhere. The average life-span of small businesses in a district of Nairobi in Kenya was just three years; according to well-informed sources, self-help projects, with their better capitalization and technical support, do not last on average much longer, though HelpAge is unwilling to provide information on this important question. When times are hard, the market may shrink, driving down the price and ruining many small enterprises. Old people may see their savings and effort collapse under conditions completely beyond their control. To the extent that self-help makes the elderly more dependent on markets and less on subsistence, it may make them more rather than less vulnerable to economic shifts they do not control.

In spite of these serious shortcomings, the self-help projects continue to offer a ray of hope in an otherwise bleak situation, where innovative government action appears remote. Because they are small-scale and relatively free from government bureaucracies, they offer a high degree of flexibility, local control, "self-determination" — and a certain degree of success, even within the uncertain terms of the market. Most importantly, they affirm the essential productive contribution that old people can make.

Given the minuscule resources that the private self-help movement has been able to mobilize, the self-help schemes should be seen realistically as models that can help shape broader policy initiatives in the future. In Costa

Rica, private organizations provide only 0.2 percent of total credit and in Bangladesh the Grameen Bank accounts for only 0.1 percent of national credit. "One of the most important roles of NGOs in this area", concludes the UN's *Human Development Report* (1993), "must be to put pressure on governments to change their policies and priorities." With major commitments of government or international funding, self-help could make a serious impact on the plight of the elderly, especially in a context of broadly expansionist economic policies.

The future of work for old people depends in the final analysis not on micro-projects, but on the global development process, its purpose and organization. If GNP growth and capital accumulation remain the benchmarks of development success, the future of the elderly will not be bright. Development must instead be defined in terms of people and their needs — especially their needs for meaningful work and adequate income. As global wealth and productivity rise, the elderly must be reincorporated into the world of work, giving society once again the benefit of their experience, their skills and their essential humanity.

NOTES

[1] The story of Uncle Lagan is told by Missori Sherman-Peters in Virginia Hazzard and Stephanie Hennings, eds., *The Elderly in the Global Community: An Untapped Resource*, New York, 1993, p.17; Grandma Migdim's story (from 1979) comes from Lila Abu Lughod, *Writing Women's Worlds*, Berkeley, 1993, pp.45f.; the story of Atorjan is taken from "Productive Ageing: A Woman in Bangladesh", *Ageing International*, March 1992, pp.24-25.

[2] Cf. David R. Phillips, ed., *Ageing in East and South-East Asia*, London, Edward Arnold, 1992, p.222; Liliana Gastron, "Le vieillissement en Argentine", abstracted in *Ageing International*, July 1992, p.15; Ken Tout, *Ageing in Developing Countries*, New York, Oxford U.P., 1989, pp.73f.; Marvin Kaiser, "Rural Elderly Benefit from International Cooperation", *Ageing International*, July 1992, p.7.

[3] Cf. Jorge Arias De Blois, *Ageing in Guatemala*, Valetta, International Institute on Ageing, 1991.

[4] According to Colin Gillion, the ILO reviewed the adverse social consequences of structural adjustment at its meetings in Geneva in November 1991, in Nairobi in October 1989, in Caracas in August 1991 and in Bangkok in November-December 1991; see his "Structural Adjustment and Social Security: The Interaction", paper presented at the Leo Wildmann symposium of the International Social Security Association, Acapulco, Mexico, 22 November-1 December 1992.

[5] *Ibid.*, p.7.

[6] "The New World of Ageing", *Ageing International*, vol. 19, no. 2, 1992, p.1.

[7] Helen Kirschner and Susan Coombs Ficke, "Senior Enterprise Development", *Ageing International*, vol. 16, no. 2, 1989, pp.24-30.

4. Family Care: Fact and Fiction

Early in May 1993, a sick elderly woman in rags was abandoned by her family on the doorstep of a local church in Kinshasa, the capital of Zaire. "This would never have happened five years ago," Zanga Yumbi, a local Red Cross official, told a *New York Times* reporter. Starving families, caught in an unprecedented economic crisis, could no longer provide for their older members.

In Santiago, Chile, a middle-class family with a shrinking income abandoned an elderly woman at an old-age home. Though Chile's economy was far more prosperous than Zaire's, cutbacks in pensions and old age benefits placed heavy new strains on families, shattering old patterns of trust and caring.

Throughout the South, the elderly face similar hardships. Economic and social crises put incredible strains on families. So do the wrenching changes from village agriculture to urban industrial life and government cutbacks in social services and pension programmes. As a result, families everywhere are weakening, and fewer multi-generational families live together or support one another. Ironically, in this time of crisis, many governments insist that families are the answer to the problems of old age, even though abundant government research shows that relatives frequently cannot and do not provide old-age security.

Families in the past varied greatly from one place to another, but they often were part of a large support network of relatives, sometimes including nearly everyone in a small village. Far fewer people then lived a long life and most were self-supporting. Those that grew frail soon died. And young children did most of the caring for dependent elderly. Generally, families held their elder members in deep esteem and kin showed support and solidarity. So the whole context of ageing was different. With the coming of urban industrial life, the meaning of "family" and the support at its disposal have changed completely.

Real families exist in bewildering variety, today more than ever before. Some embrace dozens of tight-knit kin and some are just married couples. Some have husbands with several wives and some are couples with informal or "visiting" relationships. Adult brothers and sisters may live together. Two or more women, or men, may live together in partnership. Many relatives may live together under the same roof, and husband and wife may live in separate houses. Elder support may come largely from sons, from daughters, from grandchildren, from siblings, from kin or from local chiefs. Every one of these arrangements can lay claim to being a "family", but not all are equal shelters in later life.

Family ties that protect the elderly can be very vulnerable and economic crises can quickly overwhelm and destroy them. Still, in all but the most desperate situations, families have shown great and surprising powers of survival.

Elders and the fast-changing family scene

Not long ago, experts thought that multi-generational families were on the way out, a kind of social dinosaur soon to be extinct. They were wrong: multi-generational ties have remained enormously important, in the North as well as in the South. For the elderly, in fact, families have assumed more importance as retirement or worklessness has forced them to the margins of public life.

Families can free the elderly from loneliness and a sense of uselessness, and offer them support, love and care. In return, older people can take care of grandchildren, do household chores, grow food in the garden and tend the sick. Families often share the same home, eat food together, tell stories, visit together, and rely on one another in a thousand ways.

When long-lived people reach a time of weakness and dependency, families and kin may offer them care and sustenance. Touching accounts of caring relatives in traditional villages provide inspiring ideals (and fuel for myths), as this story of an elderly African woman attests. Around 1900, as a young girl, she took care of a woman who was a neighbour and kin:

> She was very old and weak. It was my responsibility to bathe her every morning, put clean clothes on her, feed her and sit her in the sun. I then washed her dirty clothes and swept her room and cared for her throughout the day. If she needed anything, she had only to beckon.

In a more recent account from a Kenyan village, visitors to a frail family member are greeted with ceremony and courtesy:

> When visitors arrive... to pass the time with an old person, children excitedly run to announce their arrival, often waking their old relative from a nap. Tea is brought from the nearest woman's fire as a gesture of appreciation... An adult of the homestead usually remains protectively between the old person and the guests to clarify any confusion. Children gather to listen and watch and to await any errand which might arise. [1]

Today's global economic crisis makes it far more difficult for families to provide in dignified ways for their older members.

In the rural villages of China, Indonesia, Malaysia and many other countries, the majority of the world's elderly still live in multi-generational families. In rural India, the elderly normally live in families of three and four generations, averaging eight people and numbering at times twenty or thirty in all.

With the waning of the subsistence village economy, though, families have been changing. Towns and cities were first to see these changes, especially those most influenced by trade, travel and industry. In the cities of Syria, observers noticed the decline of traditional families as early as the 1920s. Large urban houses in Damascus and Aleppo had once embraced thirty or even forty family members, but by the 1950s their owners had divided them into many separate apartments. The same process was underway in the cities of Lebanon, Argentina and India. In Africa, too, family cohesion was loosening; in the early 1960s, researcher Nana Abt found that, contrary to common beliefs, many Ghanaian families were no longer supporting their elderly members.[2]

Today, as Akiko Hashimoto has shown in a unique global study for the UN University, the elderly increasingly live in diverse kinds of "families". In Zimbabwe, older people typically live in households of five — with their grandchildren but without their children (the young adults have usually migrated away). In Sao Paulo, Brazil's largest city, the elderly most commonly live alone or with their spouses.[3]

Different family arrangements offer radically different prospects of support for older people. The Indian type of village family provides the most immediate kind of support, if it isn't too desperately poor. The Zimbabwean type of family may rely on money from the missing middle generation, but the money may not always arrive. The Brazilian family may depend on government pensions, if inflation and cutbacks have not undercut this source. Given such diversity, and so many unknowns, assumptions about a standard, multi-generational family can be very misleading.

In Asia, continent of great traditional veneration towards the elderly, multi-generational living arrangements are on the wane in nearly every city — Bangkok, Canton, Manila, Bombay and many more. Less than half of China's urban older people live with their children, in contrast to more than eight in ten in the countryside. In Hong Kong, less than a quarter of older people now live with their children; and a leader of Hong Kong's elderly movement speaks of the "gradual decline" of the extended family as a guarantee of the lives of the elderly.

In Africa, because of extreme economic crisis and widespread famine and internal strife, fewer extended families remain intact in the countryside than in other continents. Families have come apart in Mozambique, Angola, Liberia and Somalia because of bloody civil wars. In Zimbabwe, only four out of ten elderly still live with children, and in some urban areas of the country half of all elderly have completely lost contact with their offspring. A third of all elderly now live alone in Kenya, according to a recent estimate. In East Africa, concludes one expert, "what is left today [of extended families] are empty sentiments which do not translate into real action".

Only two or three decades ago, in many Latin American families three generations still lived together, but now such conditions are increasingly rare.

In the Caribbean basin, where "visiting" marriages make for loose-knit relations in many families, a combination of poverty and migration has further loosened family ties. In Guadeloupe, Barbados and Jamaica, between a quarter and a half of all older people are now living alone. In Belize, fewer than one in twenty seniors live with their children and more than half live alone.

The rising tide of migration deeply erodes extended families. Young adults — unable to make a living in the village or attracted by the dreams of opportunities elsewhere — migrate to regional towns, capital cities or foreign lands, leaving behind their elderly parents and quite often their children as well. They begin by sending money or goods back home to support the family. And they pay regular visits on important holidays. A few are able to pay for a nice new house, a large farm or a television set in their native village. In the late 1980s, Egyptians working abroad sent over $3 billion a year back home, mostly to support wives, children and elderly parents, while Moroccans managed $1 billion a year.

All too frequently, though, migrants find only low-wage jobs in high-cost cities. Support payments soon fail to arrive, visits and letters stop, and elderly parents are shocked to discover that they are on their own, sole support for themselves and their grandchildren. Migrants want to be generous, for their love, their pride and their social standing are all at stake. But quite often, by the end of the month, they have nothing left.

Even when parents join their children in the city, they face hardship. In the alien, urban environment they are assaulted by strange customs, noises and life-rhythms, and bereft of their comforting village network of friends and relatives. The pattern of daily life can bring misunderstandings and clashes. In Nigeria, an aged mother who came to live with her family in the capital woke every morning at 4 a.m. and greeted all members of the family from room to room, exactly as she would do in her village. "The family could not stand the disturbance, especially on the weekends!" reported her distraught daughter. The mother soon returned to her village.[4]

Above all, older migrants are liable to feel useless and dependent. As a grown son reports from Zaire:

> It took some time for my mother to accept the fact that there was no gardening space available to her in Kinshasha [the capital city], a situation which made her feel dependent upon us. If she had been in the village, she would have been able to earn enough money to pay for most of her basic needs. At first she even resented receiving gifts and money from friends who visited her because she felt it suggested she was becoming a dependent person.[5]

The same parent eventually left her son's home — she was uncomfortable sharing his toilet after his marriage, a taboo practice in her home village.

The crisis of migration, multiplied many times, sometimes undermines an entire village economy. In one village in lower Zaire, the population fell by half over a twenty-year period and not a single young adult eventually remained — only children, a handful of teenagers and older villagers. Under such conditions, houses fall into disrepair, festivals pass uncelebrated, vital irrigation ditches fill up with soil and branches.

The elderly face an overwhelming task when the young adults leave: they must then raise the food, run village affairs, and care for the children. In spite of tremendous effort, they often cannot cope. Villages are abandoned, and agricultural production declines. Governments then reduce their rural development budget and the vicious circle continues.

The AIDS epidemic adds another harsh dimension to the family crisis. When young adults with children die of AIDS, grandparents often assume full responsibility for the care and support of the grandchildren. In parts of Zaire and other regions with a high incidence of AIDS, as many as half of all young adults may eventually lose their lives. AIDS worsens the effects of migration by depopulating the villages and concentrating all social responsibility on the elderly. If the disease continues to spread, its impact on the lives of elderly survivors — as well as children — will be incalculable.

In China, where a strict government birth-control policy has produced many one-child families, younger couples can expect four dependent parents. As life-expectancy increases, and as the age of child-bearing declines, families may include two generations of elderly as well. If generations decline in size, as in China, a forty-year old couple might be responsible not only for four older parents in their 60s, but also for grandparents in their 80s.

Cramped living quarters make matters worse. Most urban apartments or shanty-town shacks comprise no more than a single room. Many lack running water, toilets, kitchens and electricity. Family crowding in these spaces — so intense that residents barely have room to lie down and sleep — heightens tension between the generations. Often the space is simply too small to accommodate multi-generational families, no matter how tightly packed, so family separation results.

Divorce and changing values also undermine the multi-generational family. Grandchildren, imbued with new attitudes from school, radio and television, or their peers, rebel against the authority that grandparents may try to impose. Young people understandably want to escape from the power of older family members — they want to be free to choose their own friends, marriage partner, career and life-styles. Grown women also want to escape from the domination of mothers-in-law and grown men from the automatic deference they must show to their fathers.

As family members absorb the youth-centred values and age-prejudice of the urban-industrial culture, age-domination can become a tragic age-powerlessness. A writer on Bangladesh tells how family loyalty and mutual responsibility are disintegrating and the aged no longer hold on to their position of honour.

> Traditionally, aged persons held positions of honour... They made important decisions and supervised the household, enjoying physical, social and emotional security. Today, as the traditional Bangladeshi family system disintegrates, older persons are increasingly perceived as a burden.

Families generally provide far less well for women than they do for men, and myths of family care often seem to be a male invention. Elderly men are much more likely to remarry after death of a spouse or divorce — meaning that they live alone far less often. Because men frequently marry younger women, and because women are more inclined to assume caring roles, men are much more likely to get care from their spouse in later life. As multi-generational families disappear, the handicap of the woman in the "nuclear" family becomes ever more severe.

Women also are far more likely than men to assume sole responsibility for the care of grandchildren or the "old-old". In their own old age, then, they feel obliged to support not only themselves but their older husbands, older parents and young grandchildren. With less income and fewer work opportunities than men, their responsibilities for support and caring are typically far greater. This combination drives them towards poverty and increases the stress and work-load of their daily life.

Women also suffer from restricted claims to family property or use-rights to land and housing. Here, family institutions serve women badly. In most societies, women have little control over property and inheritance. When their husbands die, they often lose house, land and income to children and other relatives. A childless widow is particularly vulnerable: under law and tradition she may forfeit all her property to other relatives who may not feel responsibility for offering support.

Some countries have improved divorce laws that protect women's claim over family property, but elderly women continue to be especially at risk within the swiftly-changing family structure.

And then there are the people who have no families. In Argentina, as many as one in eight adults have no children; in Morocco one in seven are childless. Worldwide, the proportion of unmarried and childless people is on the rise. In Malaysia today about one in ten women and one in seven men are not married.

As more couples choose to have only a single child and as government birth-control programmes emphasize small families, adults are more likely to lose all their living children to war, disease or accidents, still further increasing the incidence of childlessness.

Even those with living children may have no children available for care-giving in their old age. Migration, divorce and other factors separate children from parents, decreasing the chances of care. In South Korea, about one in every seven widows now does not have a surviving son (the traditional caretaker); in just a few years, with shrinking family size and other changes, one in three will have no son to take care of them.

Ironically, the very old (who need family support the most) are least likely to have families. Because of their advanced age, children are more likely to have died or moved away, so they are far more likely than the "young-old" to live alone, without any family support.

Just because older persons frequently live with their children, their care is not assured. Many families may not have the resources to keep their elderly members well-fed and healthy. Some — occasionally through selfishness but more often out of desperation — may refuse their elders' claims to sustenance and care.

In the early 1980s, an Asian study concluded that "the elderly are finding themselves unwanted by their families". Since then, many news reports from Asian cities tell of children abandoning their elderly parents. Tragically, in the lands of "veneration", abandonment may have reached epidemic proportions, especially where poverty is severe. Even theft from elders seems to be on the rise. An elderly Turk in a publicly-supported home told how his grandson had stolen his money and furniture, leaving him without a penny and too ashamed to go back to his village.[6]

More typically, older people face resentment and emotional pressures in the extended family. Every new economic squeeze or reorganization of trade puts pressure on the elderly in larger families. They increasingly find their basic needs are not taken care of. A growing literature shows that families do not distribute resources equitably among their members and that children, women and especially old people may be at risk when times are hard.[7] One study measured the nutritional state of elderly in families in the Indonesian island of Java by measuring body mass through skinfold techniques; it found very widespread deprivation, especially in the case of a number of older women.[8]

When resources are scarce and food hard to come by, elderly may be the first to be deprived, especially if they are not able to contribute money, food, services or other essentials to the family unit. The Indonesia study found that as long as elders controlled the family budget, they got enough to eat, but when they lost control of the budget, due to age or other reasons, systematic and deep malnourishment often set in. Generally, those working most actively — especially the younger men — get the largest share of the available food.

Though Koreans traditionally treat their elders with great reverence, generational conflict has emerged as a serious problem in South Korean families. According to surveys, both older Koreans and their children increasingly prefer to live apart, and adult children are now abusing or abandoning their elderly parents. A moving television programme in 1992 told the story of a young couple who abandoned a forgetful elderly mother by leaving her on a resort island with no ID card. The lush surroundings and gay spirit of the other visitors at the resort provided a sharp contrast to the confused and penniless older woman and symbolized a rich society neglecting its older members.

Older people are most secure in families when they can make a contribution to the life of the joint household. Those who can do chores, take care of children, assist with household expenses, contribute living quarters or otherwise take a share in the support of the family tend to have the highest status and the best relations with other family members. Those who cannot make a contribution, because they are too sick or disabled, tend to lose their family position, even in cultures which traditionally venerate the elderly.

A recent survey in China shows that when the elderly cease to be productive, their status declines. The same is true for the elderly in Ghana, according to ageing researcher Nana Abt. Still, Abt emphasizes the continual contribution the elderly make in traditional Ghanaian village society. "The aged are respected because they never cease to be productive," she says. Even infirm elderly, she points out, may stay productive — consulted for their expertise in herbal medicines, religious rituals, conflict-solving and childbearing.

The China survey found that in cities as well, the quality of elderly life depended on their contribution to family support. Many elderly urban Chinese continue to work well after normal retirement age, keeping their status high and their family relations strong.

Old people's survival, self-fulfilment, respect and authority are closely tied to work and income. For this reason, the spread of the market economy and retirement are very threatening. When elderly lose their productive role in society, they lose twice over. Not only do they become poor and dependent, they also lose their position of dignity and respect in the family system.

Helping the elderly by strengthening the family

Governments often claim that families in *their* countries take good care of the elderly, eliminating the need for state-sponsored programmes. "Arabic and Islamic traditions require that parents be honoured above all worldly values," says a recent self-satisfied report to the UN from the government of Bahrain. "The family has basic responsibility for care of the elderly," states a Costa Rica white paper. Governments also insist that by centring their policy on the family, they will avoid the worst features of old age in the North, building a barrier against loneliness and abandonment.

Some governments even claim that pensions and other old-age policies undermine family care. At the world assembly on ageing, many delegates expressed this view. According to the theory, known among researchers as "crowding out", if the government takes care of the elderly, families will stop their care-giving. Most studies have shown that just the opposite ("crowding in") happens: when government pensions and other programmes ease the family burden, families carry on their caring far more effectively and may *increase* their contribution. Still, governments have persisted with the "crowding out" argument — a convenient myth to justify inaction and cutbacks in public spending. "We consider the family to be the axis of our Christian society," insisted the delegate of Chile at the world assembly on ageing, "and it is a pressing necessity to strengthen it, to support it and to help it fulfil its role in support of the elderly." This pious opinion came just a year after deep pension cuts had put unprecedented pressure on Chilean families.

Serious family support programmes make sense, by building constructively on existing institutions and traditions. But governments rarely back the programmes with adequate resources. The results have inevitably been disappointing. At best, support programmes provide a few small incentives to hard-pressed families with dependent older members. At worst, they offer nothing to families and old people except government rhetoric and ineffective legal compulsion.

In Argentina, after the collapse of the government-sponsored pension system in 1991-92, the highly-paid finance minister drew a storm of protest when he announced that henceforth families were responsible for taking care of their oldest members. During a deep economic recession, the public refused to accept this sudden redefinition of social responsibility.

Thailand's 1987-91 five-year plan reflected a similar approach. In the plan, the government drastically cut spending on social services for the elderly, while verbally emphasizing family values. The plan announced grandly that the "government will encourage... families, to recognize their role and responsibility in preventing and solving social problems".

Some governments promote family responsibility through celebrations and education, including school curricula ("moral education programmes") to strengthen traditional family values and inculcate reverence for older family members. Taiwan runs "Respecting Old People Week" and Singapore has an annual "Parent Education Programme" to "help strengthen the family and filial piety". Parades, fairs and prizes for the elderly give a festive air to these public occasions, but governments usually have a more sombre agenda in mind. "We want to teach the people that the government is not a rich uncle," said a Singapore minister recently, insisting that families must assume more responsibility for their older members. "Family life values will have to be reasserted," said a Barbados minister to a recent conference on the elderly. "We will not be able to grow old assuming that the state will provide."

Some governments back their propaganda efforts with legal compulsion, adopting laws to enforce family responsibility. In Iran, section 1200 of the civil code established the liability of children for the support of their parents. In China, even the constitution (1982) requires that "children who have come of age have the duty to support and assist their parents", and the 1980 marriage law stresses the duty of parents and children to support each other; parents who can no longer earn a living have the right to demand support from their children. Under the Chinese criminal code of 1981, flagrant violations may be punished with up to five years in prison. Cities such as Tianjin in the northeast have also passed local laws re-enforcing the national legislation.

Quite a few countries have adopted family support legislation. Tunisian law makes children responsible for housing, food and clothing for elderly parents, and Moroccan law requires children to provide food for their parents. All these laws try to codify traditional expectations, but they are also a sign that the expectations are on the wane.

The laws are not effective and they are rarely, if ever, enforced. Parents are unwilling to press support charges against their children and police prefer to avoid entanglement in such delicate family matters.

When governments provide material assistance to families, they are more likely to succeed. Even small sums can make a difference in the budget of poor families. Some countries provide income-tax deductions for children who take care of elderly parents, while others provide direct grants. Israel, South Korea, Philippines, Singapore, Lesotho, Kenya, Morocco and Malaysia are among the governments that have followed this path. Singapore, for example, provides a S$2,500 (about US$1,800) tax credit for each family with a dependent elderly person. Malaysia provides tax credits for families with elderly medical costs. Tax credits may be useful, but they favour higher-income families with large tax bills; poor families, most in need, would never benefit from the tax credit approach, since they generally pay no income tax.

Housing offers other possibilities for government family support. Hong Kong, Chile, Botswana, Brazil and a number of other countries have tried to support families through new approaches to public housing. They have built apartments large enough for extended families (previously, most apartments were too small). They have also located special units for the elderly in ordinary apartment buildings, allowing older people to live close to their children but in separate quarters. The Korean government goes further, providing small rent subsidies and housing loans for families with an older person in their care.

Numerous other programmes of family support have made a positive contribution to elderly care. "Respite care" provided by governments or volunteer organizations gives family care-givers a short vacation from their responsibilities. Home visitation services ease family burdens as well, by taking the elderly for shopping, to church or to community events. More intensive "home-care" programmes have proved best of all, by releasing family care-givers to work and so improving family income.

Programmes to encourage remarriage of widowed or divorced elderly create new family ties for those who may have lived alone. Family-centred self-help projects also bring income and new roles to elderly family members. Policies to support families vary widely, sometimes with surprising dimensions. The South Korean government even provides for a waiver of military service for an only son or for a poor young man with dependent parents.

The most effective family support programmes, such as home care, are precisely those that cost the most. Many governments simply are not willing to put up the resources to fund such programmes at the needed level. Even rich governments, with ample surpluses, have demurred. Nearly a decade after Hong Kong adopted its "care in the community", a researcher concluded that lack of funds meant the programme had "largely failed to meet its objectives".

Ironically there are also many policies with *dis*-incentives for families that live together. In quite a few countries, governments do not provide poverty relief to elderly persons living with their families, even if the families are themselves very poor. And family relief payments often decline per capita with family size. Sri Lanka's food-stamp programme, for example, discriminates quite sharply against elderly who live in large families.

Policies that increase cost pressures on families also create problems for family solidarity. The introduction of school fees, for example, because of the compulsion of structural adjustment programmes, has forced many adults to make painful choices between their children's education and support payments they were sending their parents in the countryside. Such disincentives easily outweigh special "family-support" programmes, effectively encouraging multi-generational families to divide and go their separate ways.

Governments have tried to stitch together new, artificial family units, not based on blood ties but on friendship, kindness or convenience. These are sometimes known as "fictive families". Hong Kong now allows unrelated old people to live together in public housing and so do a number of other public housing authorities. Hefei City in China's Anhui province gives families a subsidy if they "adopt" an unrelated elderly person; Argentina and other countries have recently followed suit.

Taken as a whole, government policies to strengthen families have probably made a small positive contribution to elderly lives, but they still seem pathetically meagre in view of rapid family disruption and enormous elderly need. Like self-help, family-care programmes offer interesting, locally-based solutions that can be the basis of effective policies in the future. But in the current context of cutbacks and austerity measures, they often seem more a means of deflecting public social responsibility than a serious attempt to help the elderly.

Governments and international agencies must recognize that increasing numbers of elderly will not live in families and may be cut off from family care. Neither government exhortation, nor tradition, religion and local culture will be enough to preserve and strengthen the family system if the productive potential of the elderly is not developed.

NOTES

[1] Frances M. Cox with Ndung'u Mberia, *Aging in a Changing Village Society: A Kenyan Experience*, Washington, International Federation on Ageing, 1977, p.8.

[2] Abt's research was some of the earliest work on ageing in Africa. See "The Storm Clouds are Grey", in Ken Tout, ed., *Elderly Care: A World Perspective*; and "The Role of the Family in the Care of the Elderly in Developing Countries", in Robert Kane et al., eds, *Improving the Health of Older People: A World View*, Oxford UP, 1990.

[3] Akiko Hashimoto, "Urbanization and Changes in Living Arrangements of the Elderly", in UN/DIESA, *Aging and Urbanization*, UN, 1988, pp.307-27.

[4] Cited by Mary Jo Storey Gibson, *Older Women Around the World*, Washington, International Federation on Ageing, 1985.

[5] Masamba, ma Mpolo, *Older Persons and Their Families in a Changing Village Society: A Perspective from Zaire*, Washington, International Federation on Ageing, and Geneva, WCC, 1984, p.12.

[6] Marsel A. Heisel, "Long Term Care in Turkey", *Ageing International*, June 1993, p.8.

[7] See, for example, the literature reviewed in Jodi Jacobson, "Female Poverty and the Population Trap in Urbanized Developing Countries: Issues and Prospects for Change", expert group meeting on population growth and demographic structure, International Conference on Population and Development, Paris, November 1992, pp.11-13.

[8] See Jeremy Evans, "Family Support for the Elderly in a Javanese City: A Mixed Blessing?", *Ageing International*, December 1989, 3-4.

5. Pensions and Income (In)Security

Seventy-three-year-old Paula Duarte hanged herself on a tree outside the University of Buenos Aires law school on 20 August 1992. She took her life to protest pension cuts that had forced her into destitution. In the weeks that followed, the police reported a series of such suicides.

Until the late 1980s, Argentines enjoyed some of the best pensions in the world. A special government-sponsored programme helped support the elderly poor as well. In 1949, Argentina had been the first country to include a right to pensions in its constitution. But in 1989, under pressure from the World Bank, the IMF and international lenders, the government imposed strict austerity measures, and in early 1992 it cut payments for most of Argentina's 3 million pensioners to only $150 a month, less than half the minimum needed for food and shelter.

The country's middle-class elderly — former teachers, government workers, corporate employees — found themselves suddenly among a "new poor", on the very margins of survival. Norma Pla, a leader of the pensioners' movement, reacted with outrage: "My husband and I paid social security for forty-two years. Where is that money now that we have reached old age?"

Similar cutbacks destroyed the incomes of millions of other pensioners in the 1980s and early 1990s — mainly in the industrialized countries of Latin America, where retired people had previously enjoyed the broadest and best-funded programmes. Mexico's pension fund reserves collapsed to half their former level in the decade from 1977 to 1987. Deep cuts and austerity-based reforms hit retired people in Uruguay, Chile, Brazil, Venezuela and Peru, reversing decades of pension growth.

The rise and decline of pension systems

Industrializing Latin American countries had set up pension systems long ago. Brazil established pensions for national railway workers in 1888 and broadened pensions to many other sectors in the 1920s. Argentina started a pension scheme for all government employees in 1904. Other Latin American states, including Chile, Uruguay and Cuba, followed suit in the 1920s and 1930s. Famous political leaders like Getulio Vargas of Brazil and Juan Peron of Argentina built their power with pension programmes for workers and the poor. Pensions stood among their best-known and most popular achievements.

Army officers (often influential in Latin American politics) won early and well-padded pensions. Then came civil service workers, teachers, energy and transport workers, public sector workers, and workers in private industry — usually in that order. Each new group gained its own benefit package, including health and disability insurance, financed by a separate "fund". Uruguay, with dozens of such funds, even set up a special retirement package for racetrack jockeys in the 1920s!

Sixty years later, workers in quite a few of these countries had won nearly universal pension systems. Most of the elderly depended largely on retirement monies for survival. The countries built advanced social security systems because their economies were strong, their societies quite urbanized, and their political systems responsive to pressures from trade unions, political movements and the poor. As in Europe, when older citizens were driven from the work-place, they demanded and got income support — a "social wage".

By the early 1980s, ninety countries of the South, facing similar trends of urban wage work, had adopted some kind of income-security schemes for older citizens. But most countries in Asia, Africa and the Caribbean were far poorer, more rural and less democratic than the countries with developed pensions in Latin America, and many had only recently emerged from colonialism. No powerful urban workers' movement existed to wrest pensions from the government. So most of these countries set up pitifully small pension programmes, covering adequately only the national elite — often just military officers and top civil servants. Other pensioners got only a pittance. In the Philippines, 1990 pensions paid on average just $20-30 a month — compared to the $123 that was needed, according to government figures, for a family to survive at subsistence level.

China, with its collectivist system, moved farthest to protect broad sectors of the elderly, while richer free-market urbanized countries like South Korea, Singapore and Taiwan edged only very slowly towards pensions, insisting that individual initiative and strong family values would protect their older citizens. Some prosperous countries, notably Hong Kong, refused to establish any pension system at all.

Some who retire from urban jobs return to their rural villages — a step governments often encourage to ease the pressure on city housing. Once established in the countryside, such pensioners may find their meagre stipends inaccessible. A resident of Zaire reports on his father's painful experience in the 1970s:

> The pension payment office was located 55 kilometers away from the village. With his reduced energy and deteriorating health, it took him two days to walk to the office in order to obtain his pension. If he went by truck, the only means of public transportation available in the Lukanga region, the fare would have been greater than his pension benefits. No proxy, not even that of his own children, was accepted by the pension officers.[1]

Twenty years later, with the Zairian treasury virtually empty, pensions are even harder to get. And the great majority of African and Asian elderly still have no claim to pensions, however small.

Optimists once thought that pensions would grow and spread worldwide. The ILO sponsored an international convention in 1952 that set universal standards. It drew up model pension programmes for newly-independent countries of the South. At an ILO conference in Canada in 1966, members affirmed enthusiastically that "the idea of social security already constitutes an integral part of the national conscience and its general development is an irreversible process".[2] But, unlike the richer countries of Latin America, where the pension movement was strongly-rooted in national politics, Asia, Africa and the Caribbean witnessed only slow and uneven development of income support for the elderly.

By the mid-1970s, as global economic conditions worsened after thirty years of expansion, optimism fell among policy-makers and ageing advocates. Economists recognized that growing numbers of poor elderly had not benefitted from the effects of economic growth and were condemned to destitution in the emerging world economy. But the experts were generally at a loss as to what to do. Even advocates of welfare measures, like Indian economist Amartya Sen, began to doubt whether universal Western-type social-security measures could have any relevance for poor, backward countries.[3]

Many pension programmes in the South stopped growing or began to contract. At first, economists blamed temporary setbacks like the oil crisis, the debt crisis and budget deficits. Finally some concluded the problem was permanent and structural: "excessive" numbers of elderly. By the early 1980s, experts in the rich countries began to warn that countries in the South could not afford social insurance at all, or at least that major "reforms" would soon be necessary.

In the late 1980s, the era of slumping economies and structural adjustment programmes, many of the generous pension systems collapsed. Their financial base had eroded with drastic lay-offs of workers, wage cuts and other austerity measures.

The large Latin American pension systems proved especially vulnerable. Decades earlier, at a time of far lower life-expectancy, authorities had set retirement as early as age 45 or 50, or after just 25 years of work, and they had fixed payments as a high proportion of wages. Now that people were living much longer, pension costs had risen dramatically. Active workers now had to support a larger burden of retired people. But with high unemployment, no one proposed raising the retirement age, for fear of swelling joblessness among younger citizens. Short of wider employment, there was no solution.

In the economic crunch, with government complicity, employers flouted laws mandating payments into the retirement funds — or they delayed payments to take advantage of soaring inflation. Some systems, such as that in Brazil, collected less than half the sums due, while the government did little to enforce compliance.

Corruption and bad investments sapped the pension funds as well. Millions disappeared into the pockets of politicians, union leaders and their cronies, often spirited out of the country with the help of foreign bankers. Governments forced fund managers to invest in low-interest treasury bonds that lost value in inflationary times — in effect, raising current revenues at the expense of people's future income. As official finances grew more precarious — and foreign creditors more insistent — governments dipped ever more flagrantly into the pension till.

No one in power wanted to save the pension systems through needed reforms. The military didn't want to give up their comfortable early retirements, business owners were content to keep postponing their fund payments, and politicians hoped they could go on lining their own pockets as well as financing the national treasury out of the pension system. In Colombia, when the press denounced corruption in social security, the government did not prosecute the offenders. Instead, it closed down the official inspection department!

Most pension systems laboured under extremely generous benefits for military officers and high civil servants. After the 1973 military coup in Chile, military pensions rose rapidly and the leading newspaper, *El Mercurio*, reported in 1985 that nearly two-thirds of military pensions were over 50,000 pesos, while only about one in thirty civilian pensions reached that level.

The World Bank officially disapproved of "privileged benefits". But far worse, in the Bank's view, was the "massification of privilege" — its description of decent benefits extended to ever-larger sectors of the population. "What was financially viable for a minority", complained a Bank expert, "... could not work in the long run for the mass of the insured."[4]

Beginning in the mid-1980s, under pressure from international lenders, and facing huge debt repayments, several Latin American governments with large pension programmes simply stopped making payments to their pension systems and they even appropriated pension taxes deducted from their workers' paychecks. In Brazil, pension authorities lowered benefits in order to keep the pension system solvent; they delayed paying benefits by several months, allowing rapid inflation to reduce payments to a fraction of their nominal value. In Argentina, when public authorities cut payouts, pensioners sued, charging that the government had failed to comply with the law. The government responded by declaring a "national social security emergency".

A snowball effect followed the adjustment programmes in the mid- and late 1980s, when the World Bank forced governments to reduce — often drastically — the number of workers in the public sector. Governments offered many workers early retirement, swelling the numbers of those claiming retirement benefits at just the moment the pension systems were coming under maximum stress. It is hard to imagine that the World Bank did not anticipate these results or that it did not understand how they might push the pension systems over the edge of financial viability.

While pensions declined, military and other unproductive government expenses remained virtually untouched. The World Bank and the IMF, advocates and orchestrators of the pension crises, share primary responsibility, with corrupt and irresponsible national politicians, for the pension debacle. The banks' "conditionalities" never took aim at military profligacy, or ministerial self-indulgence, or vast and growing inequalities of income, or the smuggling by corrupt officials of huge sums abroad, not to mention gigantic and wasteful public-works projects that the Bank itself promoted.

The World Bank's numerous reports on pensions ignore the human cost of pension-cutting measures. Nor do they refer sympathetically to the elderly as human beings, whose livelihood and decent treatment should be a litmus test of social policy. Instead, the Bank addresses pension issues in arcane, abstract language, full of terms like "information asymmetries", "capital market failures" and "moral hazard". The Bank refers to older people mainly as economic burdens, or dependents who no longer have anything further to contribute to the economic machine.

Trade unions, powerful forces in most Latin American countries, denounced the pension reforms and the simultaneous wage cuts brought on by the adjustment programmes. Journalists, priests, legislators all joined the chorus of protest; in 1993 the Catholic bishops in Argentina denounced the new elder poverty. But the economic crisis in Latin America was so deep and the international financial pressure so intense, that struggles by the trade unions, political parties and elderly movements did not succeed in preventing major pension cuts. Ministers of labour from across the continent assembled at a conference in autumn 1992, condemned the anti-people policies of the Bank and the IMF and called for a more humane approach to development and for new efforts to protect those hardest hit by the crisis. But the new policies remained intact.

State pensions and the alternatives

The Bank, the Fund and other financial institutions had placed the burden of the economic crisis on those with least power to resist — including especially the elderly. To justify their policy, they developed a deeply flawed analysis that placed the blame for the economic crisis on the pension systems' inefficiencies and inequities.

The right-wing Chilean government of General Augusto Pinochet, which came to power in a coup in 1973, provided the Bank with its first opportunity for far-reaching pension change. As part of a broad package of social austerity steps, Pinochet undermined one of Latin America's oldest and best-run pension systems and then totally reconstructed it in May 1981.

The Chilean "reforms" substituted privately-managed annuities (a kind of savings account), under government regulation, for public pensions. The new law required all employers to deduct 10 percent of their employees' earnings and pay the sum into these annuities operated by companies called Administradoras de Fondos de Pensiones or AFPs. Neither employers nor the government make any additional payments or have any additional responsibility, except a shaky "safety net" programme for the elderly poor. The government regulates and supervises the AFPs through a special agency called the Superintendencia.

Using the World Bank's own criteria — such as equity, protection of the vulnerable, adequacy of benefits and coverage and efficiency — the new Chilean system was in no sense an improvement on the old. In fact it was retrogressive, and led to increasing hardship for the elderly and other vulnerable sections of society.

And the Bank chose to overlook the problems in the Chilean system, and has pressed for similar "reforms" in other countries. Peru, under a new dictatorship, adopted in 1993 a plan similar to Chile's, based on what an economist calls a system of "forced personal savings" for wage-earners. Venezuela has also gone down the same path. Argentina and Mexico both introduced in 1993 mandatory savings as a supplement to reorganized and greatly reduced state-sponsored pensions.

Predictably, pensions throughout the whole region have plunged. On average in 1993, 14 million Latin American pensioners received just $132 per month, less than half the $327 requirement for "minimum necessities". In Venezuela, the average pension paid only $90 a month, while the cost of necessities stood at $185. In Peru, pensions paid $90 while necessities cost $250; in Bolivia $78 vs $307; in Colombia $123 vs $510. The *minimum* pensions were still lower: just $18 per month in Bolivia, $31 in Ecuador. The Bank had struck its blow against the "massification of privilege".

The Bank has pressed forward in spite of copious evidence in its own reports that the new systems were a heavy blow to the poorest and most vulnerable citizens. Private financial appropriation, not increased equity and well-being, appear to have been the sole guiding motive for policy.[5]

China, with the world's largest elderly population, is passing through a different but equally painful social transition on its way to a capitalist economy. Here, too, especially in the 1990s, the Bank and the Fund are actively influencing key policy decisions and presiding over yet another appropriation of pension resources.

The Chinese rural welfare system, once world-famous, went into steep decline as the government decollectivized agriculture in the late 1970s and early 1980s. Funds of the collectives had been the mainstay of support for millions of poor elderly in China's villages, people who could rely on the government guarantees for their housing, food, clothing and funeral costs. When the government introduced the current "household responsibility system", the old guarantees all but evaporated.

Regional governments and the national civil affairs ministry took up some of the slack, but far less effectively. Poor and childless elderly suffered most. By 1990, twelve years after decollectivization, only 630 out of 2000 counties had developed alternative systems of social security. At the village level, prospering new cooperative industries were able to step into the breach in some places. But because unemployment among Chinese peasants grew so swiftly and gripped tens of millions of households by the early 1990s, elder support in many families and villages fell to the lowest level in decades.

Many urban elderly in China lost out as well. Until the late 1980s, most were able to depend on relatively good pensions — about 75 percent of wages — provided by their own "state enterprise" employer. But market-driven inflation started to eat into the value of those pensions (as a Chinese saying goes: wages are dead but prices are alive). Because inflation was new, pensions were not indexed to price or wage rates.

As state firms lost government subsidies or were privatized, some went bankrupt, leaving their workers with no pensions. More commonly, firms downsized their work-force by pushing large numbers of workers into early retirement, leaving a huge load of pension costs. Amid the growing chaos, the Chinese government tried to shift enterprise-based pensions to local or regional governments, a move which in theory can provide more secure pension protection, but in practice exposes all retired people to pension cuts. Younger workers will age in a very different environment: pension rules for new private enterprises are far looser and many now offer few pension benefits at all.

The World Bank is pushing to accelerate the changes. In 1985 (just as it was getting involved in Latin American pensions) it published a study calling for pension reform in China and a move towards a national pension system. Finally, in late 1993, the Bank announced that a major loan of $600 million to China's finance ministry was under negotiation, to promote "de-linking the social responsibilities of public enterprises". The loan will cover some of the costs of transferring pensions and other benefits (like firm-owned housing) to new entities like regional pension funds or housing companies. Firms will strengthen their balance sheets and so become more attractive to private investors. Even though China's economy has been booming, pension benefits are likely to decline sharply, maybe by as much as half.

To head off a social explosion in the world's largest country, international experts are now working with the Chinese government in an intensive effort to develop a nation-wide retirement system. A host of consultants has descended on Beijing — from the World Bank, ILO, WHO, universities and private consulting firms.

Hong Guodong, one of China's most influential authorities on ageing, admits that the elderly will be asked to accept more "individual responsibility" and he insists that the government has no choice but to reduce its pension outlays. He points to the sharp drop in the ratio of active workers to elderly: from 30:1 to 6:1 in just the decade 1978 to 1988.[6] But with a plunging birthrate and far fewer children to support, the total number of "dependents" in China (children and elderly combined) has remained the same for the past ten years, a matter that Guodong and other experts have chosen to overlook.

Apparently, rural Chinese pensions will be based on individual insurance accounts, mostly funded by individual payments but with some support from local and central governments. No one has figured out how the system will work if the number of rural unemployed keeps growing. Or how people living at the subsistence level are supposed to save for the future. Experts also warn of the bureaucratic and financial nightmare of setting up this new system, covering hundreds of millions of people. Vast numbers of officials will be needed as administrators. Corruption will almost certainly take its toll. Most observers believe that in China, the elderly will pay a particularly heavy price for the new market-based approach to modernization.

In many countries all over the world, then, governments have changed pension support systems for their elderly citizens. From the harsh Chilean reforms in the early 1980s to the changes in China today, support monies in old age are at risk virtually everywhere in the South. The well-being of the elderly, as the weakest and most vulnerable, is being sacrificed on the altar of development. The World Bank and its partners have changed the rules, just when income support for older citizens is more needed than ever.

Family support as an option

Governments continue to promote "family support" as a viable option to pensions. Government ministers from Argentina to Zambia have called on families to step in and give succour to their older members in times of pension cutbacks. Governments and conservative analysts have even argued that family support is *better* than pensions, claiming that it re-enforces family unity and solidarity.

According to these theories, pensions and other forms of government support *weaken* families by undermining their mutual dependence.

But family support is often a poor substitute for pensions or other broad income-support systems. One important reason is families' inability to provide for a broad sharing of risks, like proper social insurance. People need to pool their life risks with the largest possible number of others to protect themselves against hard times. Such risk-pooling is a form of social solidarity, and it makes sense in terms of factors beyond individual control. Families provide a poor base for risk-sharing because their memberships are relatively small, and all members tend to be exposed to similar risk conditions.

Older people cannot depend on family support because too many families are just too poor and because not everyone has a family to support them. Family generosity, support and care-giving are important sources for the well-being of the elderly, but they are not a substitute for employment or a proper social insurance system.

In spite of declining family support, many parents say they want lots of children, as a guarantee of care in later life. A survey in the 1980s found that this was a major consideration for 95 percent of couples in Java and Indonesia, 77 percent in Turkey and 50 percent in Korea. These family security hopes add pressure for high birth-rates and population-related economic crises throughout the South. Policy-makers who want to check population growth may have to strengthen, not dismantle, government programmes for income-support in later life.

Many other factors affect couples' decisions on how many children to have, including cultural values and the availability of contraception. But again and again, researchers have found that young adults who feel secure about their old age are more inclined to opt for smaller families. An extensive research project funded by the ILO in Costa Rica and Thailand provides recent evidence of this.

In a recent article, Hong Guodong pointed out evidence from Muping County in China's Shandung province, where the government had recently introduced a particularly successful new rural pension scheme. According to Hong, the family planning officers in the county were surprised to find that couples' decisions on how many children to have were very quickly affected by the new pension system even though the retirement benefits were "comparatively low". Hundreds of couples who had obtained permission to have a second child voluntarily decided against conception, convinced now that their future was assured even without a male child to take care of them. [7]

Means-tested welfarism

To provide a "safety net" for the poor elderly, who have neither work nor pensions nor family support, the World Bank has proposed minimal government-sponsored payments — a kind of subsistence welfare system to prevent old people from starving to death. To qualify for these programmes, usually called "social assistance", people have to prove that they are legitimately poor — that they have neither adequate income nor assets — a process known in the literature as a "means test".

Nearly four hundred years ago, the government in England developed means-tested programmes to stave off starvation for paupers, most of whom were elderly. This system, known as the "poor laws", forced people in later life into "work-houses" — or "poor-houses" as they were later called in the United States. As poverty forced more and more people into the work-house in later life, the public eventually rejected this approach in favour of the universal pension systems we know today.

Means-test recipients often are subject to unreasonable rules. In Hong Kong, a visit to family in China for over six weeks has led automatically to a cut-off of assistance, even if a person had lived and worked in the city for decades.

By contrast, in universal programmes, citizens see their benefits as a "right" or entitlement. Even in hard times, the programmes maintain broad political support and promote social solidarity. Though even these broad programmes have come under attack and suffered cuts, they almost always provide comparatively better benefits.

Means tests have another drawback: they tend to create a large welfare bureaucracy to carry out the tests. The costs of this bureaucracy eat up a large proportion of the funds that should be going to the poor themselves. These bureaucrats often use the means tests as a tool of power — sometimes for political ends, sometimes to assert their own authority and arbitrary control.

The World Bank insists that universal social insurance is just too costly and that targetted "poverty reduction" programmes are the answer. Bank funding has supported cash grants to the poor elderly to prove this point. But the Bank's emergency programmes remain at the level of short-term "charity" and offer a poor substitute for employment, economic well-being and real social insurance. Experience with the Bank's efforts has shown that its means-tested programmes are pathetically inadequate, that they last only for a relatively brief time (often just long enough to muffle political opposition to Bank-imposed "reforms") and that they short-change the poor, in both the short and the long run.

Provident funds, other alternatives

England set up "provident funds" for urban workers in many of its poor colonies in Africa and Asia. These funds, built up by regular deductions from workers' pay, were a form of forced savings, developed as cheap options to regular pensions. Unlike a pension, the funds were available in a lump-sum payout at the time of retirement (some funds may be available even before retirement, to cover maternity leave, to finance buying a house, or to pay for the funeral of a family member). The fund payment (grown through compound interest) in theory helped its beneficiary to buy a small farm or a store or to obtain another source of income. During thirty or forty years of accumulation, the capital was available for investment to make the local economy grow.

Today, though a number of provident funds have been converted into social security systems, quite a few remain, especially in Africa and Asia (including Ghana, India, Indonesia, Kenya, Malaysia, Nigeria, Sri Lanka and Uganda). Best-known is the fund of Singapore, which covers most workers and is said to be very popular. Singapore fund accounts build up faster than those elsewhere because of high worker payments — currently more than a third of salaries — and they accumulate to a sum which is large enough to buy an annuity at retirement to support an adequate income. With a state-of-the-art electronic system, workers can check their fund totals at any time and switch their fund investments at the push of a button among a number of instruments. Singapore with its booming economy and high-tech banking system can support such a scheme, but few other countries can.

In most poor countries, provident funds are far from ideal — not just for lack of financial infrastructure but also because of the nature of the funds themselves. Usually based on a small percentage of a small salary, they rarely accumulate into a substantial sum, even after years of investment. Worse still, they are not adequately protected against inflation and often their value is seriously eroded. Paid out in a lump sum, they are all-too-often used to buy a house, take a trip or finance a daughter's wedding. They rarely provide for the real need: income security in later life.

A few countries of the South have developed income support programmes which protect their poor elderly without means testing. The programmes target those who usually are missed by wage-based pension schemes and who are typically very poor in old age — agricultural workers, small farmers, fishers, and people working in the informal sector. In 1963, the Goulart government in Brazil set up the Rural Workers' Assistance Fund (FUN-RURAL). Financed out of general government revenues, it has provided small pensions and other social coverage such as simple health care.

Though an army coup swept away the Goulart administration the year after FUNRURAL was put in place, the military leaders preserved the programme in a bid for public support. By 1975, FUNRURAL had expanded to cover not only rural workers but also domestic servants, the self-employed, small rural employers and virtually all destitute elderly, 42 million people in all — about 40 percent of the population! Several other countries in Latin America followed suit. Now, under severe austerity, the Brazilian government no longer provides adequate funding for FUNRURAL, and poverty among the elderly has seriously worsened. But FUNRURAL remains an important model for income support.

India has also pioneered in income support programmes for the elderly. There, state governments rather than the central government have taken the lead in providing income support — states with strong labour movements and powerful grassroots-based political parties. The state of Uttar Pradesh developed a general old-age pension system in 1957, and in 1961 Kerala state set up special pensions targetting widows and others likely to be destitute. Kerala extended pensions to low-income agricultural workers in 1980 — a programme that had 286,000 beneficiaries by 1986. Other Indian states, such as Tamilnadu and Maharashtra, have followed suit.

Another poor country, Gabon in Africa, has developed a special social security programme for many of its low-income citizens. Known as the national social guarantee fund, it was introduced in 1983 and covers government workers who are not covered by existing pensions, and the self-employed, including small farmers.

Mexico and Argentina also launched programmes of this kind in the 1970s, with very positive results. Mexico's COPLAMAR, with its emphasis on rural areas, was integrated with the national social security system in 1983. Researchers found that even very small payments to old people living in poor, rural areas had a big impact on their lives, since they lived partly on a subsistence basis. The grants not only helped the elderly, they improved the living standards of families and communities, too.

An important recent Indian study reaffirms the feasibility and the urgent need for government programmes to overcome poverty in old age through a serious social security safety net. It argues that means-tested anti-poverty programmes involve enormous administrative costs and that they usually fail to provide help to those most desperately in need — elderly poor. Instead, says the author, governments should expand simple, general social-security benefits to all citizens in risk categories, including widows, physically handicapped and the elderly.[8]

"Dependency ratio" and the unemployment trap

Opponents of pensions remain unconvinced by positive experiments along such lines. A common argument points to the growing proportion of elderly within the total population, especially the proportion of pensioners to active workers. This proportion, known in the technical literature as the "dependency ratio", has an aura of mathematical certainty about it that has convinced even some elderly advocates to limit their demands. The argument from dependency ratios is this: as more and more workers retire and live long lives, fewer and fewer active workers are left to support them. So the burden on the active workers and on the "economy" is becoming too great. The only solution, then, is to cut pensions or to base them entirely on personal savings.

The "dependency ratio", for all its patina of science, is actually based on a number of questionable assumptions. First of all, it counts only those considered "in the labour force" (i.e. wage workers) as non-dependent and implies that all others are somehow getting a free ride. Yet no society can function without cooking, housekeeping, child-care, care of the sick and many other humane and voluntary efforts that are not counted within the "labour force" or the "gross national product". Most women, as well as children and the elderly, become "dependents" in this scheme of things.

Work responsibilities constantly change as does the mix of ages, as economies change, urbanize and industrialize. The pension-cutters prefer to overlook these dynamics. For example, more women are working outside the home, placing more child-care responsibilities on elderly grandparents and making for fewer "dependent" younger women. And the number of children is rapidly declining, making for fewer younger "dependents" and reducing costs for food, clothing, schools, youth clubs and all the rest. In most countries of the South the number of children has declined faster than the number of elderly has grown, making for a steady decline of "dependents" from 1975 to the year 2025, according to UN projections. [9] The apocalyptic visions of the "dependency ratio" experts ignore these facts.

Most important of all: many "dependents" would like to have jobs in the wage sector but cannot find them. The great majority of urban elderly are frustrated job-seekers, who — by all accounts — would prefer employment to impoverished retirement. So when World Bank policy-makers coolly deny millions of people jobs on the ground that the market does not need them and then deny them the most basic income support because the "dependency ratio" is too high, they play a cruel, self-serving and irresponsible ideological trick. The "dependency ratio" — if it has any reality — is the result of mass unemployment and structural adjustment, not uncontrollable population shifts. The Bank's neo-Darwinian policy jettisons the weakest and makes their suffering a precondition for the prosperity of a few.

Pension-cutting is outrageous. But pensions and other income-security systems have a fatal flaw. They tend to legitimize the concept of "old age" and the expulsion of people from wage work, irrespective of physical abilities, personal preferences and capacities for productive social contribution.

The challenge is how to combine basic income security with the right to stay productive in wage work or be rewarded for productive but unpaid work (like taking care of grandchildren). Remunerated work not only would benefit the elderly, but also would put their talent and labour more fully at the service of society. Full employment (in a new and expanded sense, for all those who can and wish to work) must become the foremost priority for ageing advocates.

But what about those who are too infirm to work, or who cannot find productive and paid labour? In an increasingly global economy, where the fates of all are closely intertwined, and where individual nation-states are often too weak to protect their own citizens, a global solution to income security is needed, including support for people in frail old age. Arthur H. Westing, in a book published by SIPRI in 1988, was one of the first to propose an international social security system, based on a worldwide tax.[10] As the global economy becomes more and more productive — and less and less dependent on labour — the need to distribute the social wealth in radically new ways becomes ever more pressing. And the claims of the impoverished elderly become ever more urgent and compelling.

The tradition of social solidarity in pension and income-security systems remains a powerful force, which is likely to attract increasing support in the decades ahead. The great flaw of age discrimination in employment must be eliminated as income-security for all is rethought. Justice requires new projects to support and broaden income-security systems throughout the South — projects which are not designed with mere survival in mind.

Three initial steps are necessary. The global economy must engage the productive capacity of all and provide everyone with a decent sustenance. Serious reforms that strengthen public income support and pension schemes are urgently needed, including better and more honest administration, rigorous collection of taxes, inflation-indexed payments, and the like. And pensions and income support guarantees should be extended to wider categories of the population, including agricultural workers, domestic workers and the self-employed, so that coverage will eventually reach the entire population. Broadening coverage for women, including those who work in the home, is especially important.

These steps presuppose changes in the international economic order, including rethinking the role of the World Bank and the IMF with their extremely narrow definition of economic success and development. Globalization of employment and income security, for people of all ages, is the only way to ensure a decent livelihood and opportunities for productive work to everyone, the elderly included.

84

NOTES

[1] Masamba, *op. cit.*, p.15. Note that walking 28 kms (18 miles) per day is considered the result of physical handicap for a rural Zairian. Western hikers, in good physical condition, would be quite content with such mileage.

[2] Ottawa Programme of Social Security Reform for the Americas, as quoted in ILO, *Report of the Director-General*, Geneva, 1992, p.65.

[3] See commentary on Sen in S. Guhan, *Social Security for the Unorganized Poor*, Bombay, 1992, pp.9-10.

[4] Carmelo Mesa-Lago, *Social Security and Prospects for Equity in Latin America*, Washington, World Bank, 1991, p.85.

[5] The entire restructuring of pensions can best be seen as a very large appropriation in favour of foreign debt holders. No one has estimated the size of the sums involved, as far as we know, but conservatively the total must be at least $56 billion on a capitalized basis. If we assume that 14 million pensions were reduced to $1,584 on an average of, say, $200 apiece, we arrive at $2.8 billion annually or $56 billion if capitalized at 5 percent. The overall reduction was probably far higher than the $200 figure, yielding a capitalized sum of as much as $200-300 billion.

[6] Hong Guodong, "Support for the Elderly in China: Gradual Improvements in Social Security", in Tarek Shuman et al., eds, *Population Ageing: International Perspectives*, San Diego, 1993, p.435.

[7] *Ibid.*, p.440.

[8] S. Guhan, *op. cit.* For the case of Tamilnadu, see pp.14-23; for the all-India proposal, see pp.23ff.

[9] See United Nations Office in Vienna, *The World Ageing Situation 1991*, pp.35-36.

[10] Arthur Westing, ed., *Cultural Norms, War and the Environment*, New York, Oxford, 1988, p.157. Westing argues that population issues are connected to the security of old age and that supporting older people is therefore intimately connected to checking population growth.

6. Health Care and Wellness

Gaunt, motionless elderly, bony old beggars and aged garbage-hunters testify throughout the South that hunger and malnutrition are the greatest threats to the health of older people. Hungry people simply cannot be healthy, and poor elderly are very likely to be hungry. Single and abandoned elderly run the greatest risk of hunger. Even in families, the elderly are usually first to go hungry and last to get nutritious foods.

More than half of all older people in the South probably lack the food they need for an active existence — including self-care and elementary social contacts, according to estimates by the Food and Agriculture Organization and the World Bank. Under-nourishment leads to depression and listlessness, as hungry people lose hope and interest in life. They may even lack the energy to get food, water, firewood and other basic means of life sustenance. Yet there is enough food in the world to feed everyone.

Even the elderly who get enough calories often suffer from an unhealthy diet — from deficiencies of vitamins and minerals necessary for physical fitness. Most common are shortfalls in iron, calcium, iodine or vitamins A and C. These and other "micronutrient" types of malnutrition can strike those who live mainly on potatoes, bread or rice. Micronutrient malnutrition affects twice as many people as hunger. Perhaps three quarters or more of elderly in the countries of the South suffer from its effects, simply because they cannot afford to eat properly.

In some field surveys, researchers have expressed surprise that older people can survive at all, given the very small amount of food they eat. Often, a third to a half of the elderly report eating only one meal a day or less. In an urban township in Zimbabwe, half of the aged had no regular income and "it was not uncommon to find them having gone without food for one or two days".[1] Elderly living with families are commonly malnourished as well. In Inaon, a Philippine village where every older person lives with families, more than 8 in 10 were found to have less food than basic subsistence required. WHO data show that diet-related deaths due to non-communicable diseases increased sharply over the past thirty years in most of 42 poor countries studied. In some countries — including Egypt, Ecuador and Thailand — such deaths more than doubled.

When Southern governments take steps to improve health, they rarely pay much attention to malnutrition. Health ministries do not consider themselves responsible for food. Doctors mention diseases, not hunger, as causes of illness and death. Even WHO did not mention hunger in its big multi-country elder health survey.

Until recently, many governments promoted food consumption, by fixing a low price for staple foods and cooking fuel. These price controls, and the government subsidies that went with them, kept essential commodities accessible even to the very poor. Over the years, governments set up other programmes to reduce starvation and malnourishment — such as free distribution of food or food-for-work schemes. As a result, famine and mass starvation are far less common than they once were.

During the 1980s, though, structural adjustment programmes eliminated many nutrition-support schemes, especially price controls for food. The World Bank believes that subsidies distort market forces and burden government budgets, so they must be cut. The Bank forced governments to lower and eventually end subsidies, allowing food prices to rise to world market levels. Prices of essential food items — such as bread, flour, rice and cooking oil — sometimes doubled overnight, putting them out of reach of the poor.

Sri Lanka came under the Bank's scalpel. In January 1978, the IMF and the World Bank forced the government to reorganize and cut spending on the country's very successful food-aid programme. At first, the government restricted eligibility to the most destitute. Then it held spending down while inflation rose, effectively cutting the value of aid. Between 1979 and 1980, food-aid fell to only a seventh of its former level.

As austerity-created hunger spread across the South in the 1980s, the World Bank and the IMF came under heavy criticism from international humanitarian organizations and from political groups in the affected countries. The Bank then introduced what came to be known as "safety net" programmes. A portion of Bank lending supported efforts to "ease the burden" of adjustment shocks on the most vulnerable citizens. In practice, these programmes fell far short of their goals.

Typically, under pressure from UNICEF, the safety nets included programmes to sustain nutrition in mothers and children. But the Bank had no programmes that specially targetted older people. One survey in the mid-1980s found that only 8 out of 47 developing countries had nutritional programmes directly for the hungry elderly.

Jamaica's "safety net" — like many others — failed to protect its most vulnerable citizens. Its food aid programme, introduced in 1984 under a structural adjustment agreement, targetted a million people, or half the population of the country. The programme offered cash grants to the very poor of all ages to offset rising food costs. But the cash stopped in just a few months when the government ran out of funds. Restarted a year later, the grants quickly eroded under inflation. Even at its peak, the programme covered only a fraction of the needy population.

Other countries, from Brazil to Zambia, have tried to grapple with hunger under very unfavourable international circumstances. They have set up soup kitchens, wholesale food programmes for poor families, and new "food-for-work" schemes. Other approaches have tried to help farmers raise food production, improve local food storage and transport, and ensure its consistent availability in the market.

Self-help projects for the elderly have often aimed at stabilizing or increasing their food resources. Gardens, backyard animals and fruit trees — staples of self-help — have assisted the elderly to provide for their own food needs. Hydroponic gardens in the Dominican Republic, fruit trees in India, and backyard rabbit-raising in Peru — all moderate but do not stop the rising pressures of malnutrition on the elderly.

Some governments and NGOs have even set up urban centres for the poor elderly that provide free or low-cost meals. In Madras, India, older members plan, buy, cook and serve hundreds of meals each day in one such centre. The grandmothers club in Lima, Peru, run by elderly women, prepares daily meals for 120 older people. But nutritional programmes cannot offset the combined effects of structural adjustment, concentration of land ownership, urbanization and environmental degradation. The FAO warns that food production may even decline in some countries in the years ahead, partly because of competition from foreign grain imports. So the elderly remain at high risk and they may get hungrier unless urgent action is taken.

In December 1993, WHO and FAO held a joint international conference on nutrition in Rome. The gathering helped spotlight the connection between health and hunger and it produced new commitments to increase poor people's access to food. Unfortunately, the issue of nutrition for the elderly drew little attention, and no special emphasis on elderly nutrition emerged.

A WHO study concludes that "in times of increased economic hardship, famine and civil disturbance, the elderly in underprivileged populations suffer disproportionately..."[2] Professional services like doctors, hospitals or even primary care clinics cannot effectively promote health under such conditions.

Old people will not be well and cannot contribute effectively to society unless they have better access to work, income, food, housing and sanitary conditions. No hospitals or health professionals can provide these needs, which are rooted deep in the global economic system.

Health services: an era of cutbacks

Anum Tetteh had badly swollen legs — so bad he couldn't walk. Getting on in years, he lived in a small wood shack in Accra, the capital of Ghana, with his brother, his niece and her children. As time passed, Anum's health steadily worsened. He wanted to consult a doctor, but he could not afford the public health service fee. Since the family had barely enough money to buy food, nothing was left over to cover Anum's check-up. So he stayed at home, agonizing, getting sicker, waiting to die.[3]

Structural adjustment forced Ghana's government to charge fees in 1983 for its formerly free public health service. Further pressure led to sharp fee hikes in 1985. More than half the former patients stopped coming to the health clinics. Poor elderly cut back the most.

Ghana's health system nearly collapsed in the budget squeeze of the late 1970s and early 1980s. Buildings deteriorated, equipment broke down, drugs were no longer available. Hundreds of demoralized doctors and other health professionals left the country. WHO sharply criticized the World Bank for these drastic austerity measures, saying that they "focused too closely on money" and not enough on "the inevitable health and human consequences".[4]

In similar circumstances around the world, millions of elderly lost access to health care. In just eight years, after steep budget cuts, patient consultations in the public-health service of Senegal dropped by four-fifths. One-third of Asian and Latin American countries reduced their public-health budgets. Thirty-seven of the world's poorest countries cut their health budgets by half, with Africa hardest hit. Even China, long a leader in rural health initiatives, downgraded its simple medical assistance programme in the countryside.

WHO researchers, taking account of rising populations and soaring numbers of elderly, believe that health spending per capita has declined in nearly every country of the South. A third or more of all medical equipment is now unusable and drugs as basic as aspirin are commonly missing in primary-care clinics for months at a time.

Even in the richer countries, cutbacks left the public health systems reeling. In most countries of Latin America, hospitals stopped serving meals, supplies of basic medicines ran out, and patients even had to provide their own syringes, gauze and other basic surgical materials![5] Most alarming of all, as the public-health sector declined, preventive health efforts slowed down. Infectious and parasitic diseases like malaria and tuberculosis returned. The elderly, more exposed than others, had less chance of getting medical aid. Those who kept their place in line often had to make heavy sacrifices. WHO reports that in recent years many elderly desperately sold their house or their farm, or went deeply into debt, just to pay fees for private care. In China, where health care used to be free, poor rural elderly referred to city hospitals run the risk of financial disaster, according to a 1993 report by the Amity Foundation. Rising hospital and transportation costs, the report states, "often run the family into poverty and deeply into debt".

Rather than restoring health services for the elderly, many governments plan to reduce them further, on grounds that scarce resources are "wasted" on the old. The Pan American Health Organization (PAHO) warns in a recent publication that market-based health planning, with its emphasis on "cost-benefit" analysis and economic productivity, has fostered this attitude. According to Dr

Elias Anzola, director of its elderly health programme, progress in elder health reform has been largely blocked by "those who question the economic rationality of measures that assign resources to solving the problems of a 'non-productive' minority".

Budget-cutting economists and health officials often insist that health care for the elderly eats up a larger proportion of health spending than care for those of any other age group. A recent study in Thailand concluded that those over 60 used four times as much medical resources as those of other ages. And a study in Costa Rica found that those over 60 visited hospitals and consulted doctors twice as frequently as the average for the population as a whole.

Many studies support the view that rising numbers of medically-hungry elderly will cause a ruinous increase in overall health-care costs. The argument runs like this: As public-health measures bring infectious and parasitic diseases (like cholera, malaria and tuberculosis) under control, chronic diseases (like cancer and heart disease) — which mostly affect the elderly — are increasing. Chronic diseases often call for expensive medical interventions involving hospitalization and even surgery, diverting resources from urgent measures of child and maternal care and other more "cost-effective interventions".

These explanations seem plausible, but are terribly misleading. Everyone agrees that older people need more health-care attention than younger citizens, even under ideal conditions. But in many third-world countries, a big share of health-care costs is consumed by a small number of the most privileged urban-dwellers — government officials, wealthy bankers and merchants, high-ranking army officers and their spouses. The fact that many of these patients are elderly does not change the pattern of discrimination which denies care to the great majority of older citizens.

Many countries spend half or more of their entire public-health budget on a handful of big-city hospitals; more than one-fifth of their public health allotment typically goes to support just one teaching hospital. The overwhelming majority of elderly citizens lose out from this deployment of health-care resources.

Primary care for the elderly

WHO began to promote more equitable health-care delivery at a major 1978 joint gathering with UNICEF in the central Asian city of Alma Ata. The assembly criticized hospital-centred Western models of health care and proposed a focus on primary health care, based in local communities. The "primary care" model meant emphasis on prevention and on maintenance of wellness — rather than curing sicknesses. The Alma Ata assembly also proclaimed an ambitious goal: "The attainment of all peoples of the world by the year 2000 of a level of health that will permit them to lead a socially and economically productive life." The elderly stood to gain a great deal from these reforms, but implementation has been disappointing. Northern-inspired, curative medicine has everywhere been in the ascendancy.

Exceptions stand out. Costa Rica and Cuba led the way in Latin America while Sri Lanka, Malaysia and China set the pace in Asia. In Sri Lanka (before recent cuts) more than nine out of ten citizens had access to health care and the elderly were found to live far healthier and longer lives than their South Asia neighbours.

In the years since Alma Ata, a few governments have shifted spending towards primary care, and most health services have embraced initiatives like mobile health units (clinics on wheels) for rural areas. The World Bank, while arguing for "market"-based health reforms, complains about continuing maldistribution of health resources. Ironically, until very recently its own programmes — and those of its most influential members — continued to promote medical technology and hospital construction to boost industrial countries' export markets. The medical profession, deeply influenced by medical practice in the rich countries, has often been a barrier to reform, too, since doctors tend to make far more money in clinically-oriented, hospital-based health systems than in those devoted to prevention and wellness. As a result, progress since Alma Ata has been uneven at best.

Geriatrics and health programmes for the elderly

About the same time as Alma Ata, international health organizations took up the issue of "ageing". In 1980, PAHO put ageing on its agenda and WHO launched a number of important studies of elder health. National health ministries set up small but promising programmes in this field.

WHO decided on a fourfold approach to elder health care: (1) to bring the special needs of the elderly into the regular work of community health programmes; (2) to organize regular health screening clinics for the elderly, so that medical personnel could see them on a regular basis and detect illness earlier; (3) to improve elderly access to care by using more mobile units; (4) to train family members in how best to care for older parents and relatives.

There have been positive steps in response to these initiatives, but few countries implemented the basic concepts in their health programmes, and they remain largely a dead letter. WHO continues its efforts to promote elder health. It lobbies for inclusion of geriatric courses in medical training, it pushes for elder programmes in community-health systems and it carries out promising research — especially a major current study on the causes of elder wellness, called the "determinants of successful ageing". Unfortunately, WHO has trimmed its already scant budget for this programme. Only two professional staff worked on global elderly health issues in 1993 at WHO headquarters in Geneva, and by 1994 one had left and not been replaced. In PAHO, the most active regional programme, a single professional worked only part-time on elderly issues.

Disabilities

About ten percent of those over 60 in the South have major disabilities — like blindness or extensive mobility loss — and a quarter of those over 80 are seriously disabled. Any programme to improve the health of the elderly must focus on disability issues, yet in most countries disabilities rate a dismally low priority.

In Nigeria, a third of those over 60 have vision problems and the same is true in nations of the Western Pacific and in Latin America. Between a quarter and a half of the elderly have lost most of their teeth. And about one in ten have serious problems with hearing and mobility. Altogether, about half of all older people have some kind of disability and about a quarter face real limitations in their daily life as a result.

Health professionals and policy planners often look on disabilities of the elderly as unavoidable — a kind of expectable body decay. But most disabilities are preventable. And many can be cured or eased with simple and inexpensive devices like eye-glasses or dentures.

Fortunately, some disabilities are on the wane. WHO campaigns have reduced blindness, especially trachoma, river blindness and other eye diseases — mainly by eradicating disease-carrying insects and purifying drinking water. At the same time, though, overall disabilities have risen in virtually every country from Bangladesh to Turkey. Health experts see a number of causes: people are living longer, nutrition has worsened, and health-care systems have deteriorated. Disabilities are also on the rise from motor vehicle accidents, industrial accidents, pollution and social violence — the direct results of "development". Elderly are often the first victims of these causes: they are most likely to be hit by cars and trucks, more vulnerable to the effects of air pollution, more exposed to nutritional shortfalls.

In disability treatment, the biggest advances have overcome blindness and serious visual impairment, especially through use of cataract surgery. Governments and citizen groups have organized huge campaigns of eye-care education and treatment. India adopted a national plan to reduce blindness in the late 1970s and over a ten-year period operated on nearly 10 million people and put in place an enormous eye-care and education system. The Blind Men's Club, a private citizens group, participated actively in the campaign with assistance from HelpAge International, sending mobile cataract teams to thousands of villages and sponsoring a very effective programme in rehabilitation. International and local efforts to fight blindness go forward on every continent, under the sponsorship of groups such as the International Eye Foundation and the Caribbean Council for the Blind.

But other kinds of prevention or treatment have made little progress. WHO concedes that effective dentistry is non-existent in most public-health programmes. So people continue to believe that when a tooth hurts it should be pulled out. In the countryside, many older people have lost most teeth by the time they reach 60, so they often have serious problems eating — and even talking.

Beyond prevention and cure, devices like eyeglasses, hearing aids, wheelchairs, dentures and prosthetics (artificial arm, leg, etc.) can be of enormous help to the disabled. These are all too rare in the South, with the exception of wheelchairs, commonly made locally from bicycle wheels attached to ordinary chairs, and simple prosthetic devices, usually carved from wood.

Human service agencies in the industrial countries send used eye-glasses to third-world countries; the Lions Club in the US has a programme of this kind. Simple non-prescription eye-glasses, such as those available in drug stores, could be made available by public health services. Braces, crutches and other inexpensive devices could be distributed, too, with enormous results in the well-being of the disabled, most of whom are elderly. Expensive devices like hearing aids or quality dentures are likely to take lower priority as long as resources are scarce.

WHO has also tried to emphasize rehabilitation and community education as approaches to disability. Rehabilitation seeks to help the disabled to regain some or all of their lost function, or at least to help those who have lost functions to learn how to cope. Community education and advocacy help train family and friends to be more effective sources of support and care-giving and to over-come the strong stigma of being disabled. Excellent as these plans are, they are only very rarely put into practice.

Health care "reform" and structural adjustment

Beginning in the mid-1980s, the World Bank pro-posed structural health "reforms" — in addition to its stock-in-trade budget cuts. Often, the Bank made the reforms a condition of its assistance loans. Governments had little choice but to accede. The new Bank programmes called on governments to allow unrestricted development of private, fee-for-service health care. They insisted that public-health authorities widen the application of "cost recovery" fees and raise prices for consultations, treat-ments and the distribution of medications. And they insisted that governments promote semi-public or private health insurance systems as an alternative to public tax-funded care. Bank experts argued that curative health care was essentially a consumer commodity, best allocated by private markets to all but the very poor.

These reforms are of doubtful value, especially for the elderly, with their chronically low income. Increasingly, experts agree that most citizens in the South have neither the information and the money nor the desire to "consume" health care like toothpaste, soap or sneakers. As marketized health providers concentrated on upscale markets, the oldest and those with most need for care have been the first to suffer.

Stung by a mounting chorus of criticism, the World Bank in the late 1980s began to insist that "targetted poverty-reduction" stood at the centre of its structural reforms of health care. Bank experts argued — as they did with pensions — that public-health spending failed to reach the poorest citizens. Those with higher incomes, they claimed, should pay for their care and public spending should be focused on the very poor.

For all the talk about "poverty reduction", though, the Bank's reforms forced most countries to cut back sharply on medical services to the poor. Mexico cut in half its health services to the rural poor in the years 1982-1986 alone, while measures of "decentralization" shifted health expenses from the central government budget to hard-pressed and unprepared local governments, sharply lowering the quality of service. The results were similar in Brazil's FUNRURAL programme for the poor and the peasant social insurance in Ecuador.

In the course of adjustment programmes, Latin American countries also suffered blows to social-insurance-based health systems: as their pension funds fell into crisis, the related health funds ran short of resources also. In Mexico and Argentina, authorities cut pensions and health-care services at the same time. Costa Rica managed to preserve the essentials of its excellent health system, with entitlement for nearly nine out of ten older citizens, but with a sharp decline in service.

Perhaps the most alarming "reform" took place in China. Most elderly Chinese live in the countryside and until recently they depended on health care organized by local agricultural collectives known as brigades. Each year families paid a small part of their rice production to support the expenses of the local primary-health clinic. This system worked so well that health improved dramatically and people in China now live nearly as long as citizens of rich countries. But when China decollectivized agriculture in 1979-85, it shifted rural health to a fee-for-service basis. Instead of an annual insurance fee, payable in kind, patients had to pay in money for every consultation, and emphasis shifted from prevention to cure. Many, if not most, older people simply could not afford the new system. Fees in China skyrocketed from 19 percent of total health financing in 1980 to 44 percent in 1985. Even though incomes rose for many peasant families during this period (other families got poorer), most of the former "barefoot doctors" and other practitioners could not survive on a fee-for-service basis. They left the countryside and local clinics closed for lack of funds. In Sichuan province, more than half the villages now lack a clinic. Care is miles away. The whole Chinese rural-health system has deteriorated drastically.

A sharp rise in tuberculosis revealed China's market-based health crisis. Under the new fee-based system, patients could not possibly afford expensive TB drug treatments costing $30-80 each. As a result, several thousand — many of them elderly — died unnecessarily, a million or more remained infected, and tens of millions of people became newly-infected. The government had to revise its policy to head off a full-scale epidemic. Now, government subsidies ensure that all can be treated. But the decline in China's remarkable health programme has not been reversed.

It would appear that the World Bank has been writing off the elderly. Though the Bank has never articulated an expressly anti-elderly programme, its reform priorities and its publications increasingly reveal a deep bias against health care for older people. The Bank's major report *Investing in Health* (1993) provides the clearest evidence. An elaborate cost-benefit analysis seeks to identify the most effective health "interventions" and this analysis is based on a table assigning different "values" to life at different ages. The values appear to be determined almost completely by a person's role as a worker. By the Bank's reckoning, the value of a life at age 25 is more than twice the value of a life at age 70 and nearly three times the value of a life at age 80. Even simple and inexpensive care for the impoverished Southern elderly would be hard to justify under such criteria. No wonder, then, that *Investing in Health* never once addresses the special issues and needs of elder care.

The role of religious and citizen organizations

In the face of Bank-induced cutbacks, hard-pressed governments have called on international religious bodies and secular citizen groups for help. Christian missionaries had set up the first hospitals in many African and Asian countries, but post-independence governments saw these as part of colonialism and frequently took them over. Today, the churches' role in health — particularly in Africa — is again on the rise.

In a time of cutbacks and privatization, many governments see private groups as more effective health-providers than bureaucratic and sometimes corrupt public institutions. A number of African countries — including Malawi, Uganda and Zambia — are so keen to encourage private efforts that they subsidize church hospitals and clinics and underwrite the training of their health personnel. This partnership of governments and private non-profit groups has worked relatively well and is sure to expand in the future.

Citizen groups have often been more experimental in health services to the elderly than government agencies. Churches may have an advantage when they are committed to serve the downtrodden and connected to grassroots community movements. Both Catholic and Protestant groups have organized the most effective local health services for the aged and the poor in the slums of Mexico City, using volunteer assistance from physicians and other health workers. Churches and ecumenical groups have pioneered in bringing health to the elderly in dozens of villages in India. A Methodist group piloted the Hong Kong community nursing centre. The Amity Foundation is an important church-supported group working to shore up the faltering primary-care system in China. The list is long and the achievements impressive.

Secular groups can enjoy similar service advantages. HelpAge International has introduced health initiatives for the elderly in many lands, from new eye-treatment facilities in Somalia to primary care in India, and it has produced an important handbook on elderly health.[6] But private non-profit organizations can also be bureaucratic and conservative. Churches are still inclined to spend money on building and running hospitals, rather than primary-care programmes. They are more likely to build traditional nursing homes than train community care-givers. By acting to please church members and donors in distant lands, they often fail to meet the needs of the people they set out to serve. Church-based programmes that depend on local governments for funds may also become prisoners of conservative government priorities. And they are rarely in a position to survey and plan for country-wide needs.

At their best, churches and citizen groups serve as pioneers and advocates, rooted in local needs. The Hong

Kong community nursing programme shows the potential but also the limits of this approach. Started entirely privately by a local Methodist group, it established a need and paved the way for effective service. Today, more than twenty years later, other churches and non-profit providers have joined the effort. To make the expanded service possible, all receive support from the Hong Kong government. None feels free, though, to criticize the government for failing to serve more than a small percentage of the community care need, nor to speak out on larger issues of elder survival and care.

Traditional medicine and the elderly

Traditional cures, still part of life in most countries of the South, have much to contribute to the health of the elderly. In fact, with Western-based medicine so expensive and inaccessible, older people have little choice but depend on the traditional cures provided by herbalists, acupuncturists and other local specialists of the healing arts.

Western medical professionals long scorned these kinds of care, but today some public-health experts recognize their value and effectiveness. In 1985, WHO held its first international meeting on traditional medicine and the organization now has a special programme in support of traditional health practices. It has evaluated herbal and acupuncture methods and developed a manual on traditional medicine.

Traditional healers are often themselves elderly, expressing the respect village culture usually gives to old people for their wisdom, authority and magical powers. Traditional healing, then, is a form of employment and affirmation for the elderly, and recognition of their special knowledge. Some experienced Chinese herbalists know thousands of different herbal remedies and stock many hundreds of herbs in their simple village shops. In Africa, the oldest woman in the family often assumes responsibility for keeping track of the more common herbal remedies — like "fever leaf" for malaria and "jalobo" for jaundice. Bonesetting is a separate and quite common specialty. So is midwifery. Acupuncturists, yoga masters, hot bath therapists and others offer treatments that ease pain and help the body produce its own cure.

Traditional medicine may not have the curing powers of Northern medicine when faced with life-threatening illness, but in many circumstances it offers effective treatment at small cost. So effective is the treatment, in fact, that citizens of rich countries sometimes seek these cures out of preference, not financial necessity.

Some governments — especially those in China, India, Nepal and Sri Lanka — have long supported traditional medicine and integrated it into their village-level primary-health system. From all evidence, the elderly have especially welcomed these programmes.

Ways forward

Thanks to improved sanitation and public-health measures, elderly health has improved dramatically over the past fifty years. Longer lives and fewer contagious diseases prove this progress. But in the last ten years, while world resources have grown, elderly health has worsened in many lands. As public-health budgets and food support programmes have been cut, illness, disability and mortality are rising among older people.

Progress will require a reversal of these recent trends as well as a much greater commitment to international programmes in elder health, especially through WHO. Governments and international agencies will also have to address environmental causes of elderly ill-health, ranging from vehicle safety to industrial pollution to urban stress.

Dozens of creative initiatives in many countries point ways forward — from traditional healing, to community control, to research into the determinants of healthy old age. Slowly, and often in the teeth of opposition from the medical establishment, governments and citizen groups are insisting on broadening training in medical and nursing schools to include care for the elderly. New institutions are training health professionals in preventive work, especially work to promote wellness among the elderly and to encourage families and communities to offer appropriate kinds of care to the sick and the infirm. Special initiatives to overcome disabilities, particularly blindness, are offering prospects of a fuller life to many elderly.

In many countries, governments and citizen groups are setting up daily exercise programmes for older citizens, stressing proper diets, and working more effectively to discourage smoking and abuse of alcohol and drugs. Citizen groups and older citizens have set up networks of home care, have lobbied for cheaper, generic medicines and have worked hard to make bureaucratic health systems and hospitals more responsive to the needs of elderly patients. Efforts to support informal care-givers and to help people take care of themselves are among the most important emerging programmes. Emphasis on women's health in later life has emerged as a new focus of care. Elderly people themselves are often the main organizers and volunteers, providing an important gesture of elder-elder solidarity.

NOTES

[1] Joe Hampson, *Old Age: A Study of Aging in Zimbabwe*, cited in *Ageing International*, vol. 10, no. 4, winter 1984, p.6.

[2] A. Horwitz et al., *Nutrition and the Elderly*, Oxford, Oxford University Press, 1989, p.10.

[3] Karl Maier, "Economics of New Era Unravels Africa's Safety Net", *Washington Post*, 21 July 1992.

[4] WHO, *World Health Situation*, 1993, p.89.

[5] Carmelo Mesa-Lago, *Social Security and Prospects for Equity in Latin America*, Washington, World Bank, 1991, p.115.

[6] See Gill Garrett, *Adding Health to Years: A Basic Handbook on Older People's Health*, London, HelpAge International, 1993.

7. Older Women at Risk

In all countries of the South, older women are especially vulnerable among the elderly population. They are far more likely than older men to have lost their spouses and to lack secure opportunities for work or sustenance. They are also more likely to lack ownership of land or a home, to carry responsibility for the care of others, and to be poor.

Lamila, 69 and living in an African town, is typical of those at greatest risk. Sick and nearly destitute, she lives alone. Years ago, two husbands divorced her because she could not bear children. Now her brother is dead, her sister lives at a distance and she has no children to help her out. She scrapes a living selling fried plantains, but seldom has enough to eat. Often too weak to fetch food, water or other necessities, she must beg the neighbours' children to help her.[1]

Women live longer than men, and among the very old women outnumber men by a wide margin. Women live about a year longer in India and Egypt, three years longer in China and Ethiopia and more than six years longer in Guyana and Uruguay. In China and Brazil, women aged 80 and over outnumber men by about two to one. As economies become more industrialized and more completely absorbed into market capitalism, women's life-expectancy grows faster than men's, for reasons that are not well understood. Worldwide, women are a growing proportion of all elderly people. So the issue of ageing is more and more a women's issue.

At first glance, longevity may seem an advantage, but in practice it often is not. Far more likely than men to be poor and chronically ill, many women find old age difficult at best, far from a blessing. A lifetime of gender disadvantage shapes a woman's condition in old age, making self-support especially difficult. Girls get less education and training than boys and they often marry very early. Even today in villages across the South many women are married by 15 or 16.

Women assume life-long responsibilities for nurturing and caring for family members: child-rearing, domestic chores and nursing the sick. These responsibilities keep them from developing literacy, from gaining employment-related skills, and from working for wages outside the home. In countries as diverse as China and Tunisia, men over 60 are five times more likely to be literate than women.

In most countries of the South, men hold the overwhelming majority of skilled jobs, from mechanic to medical doctor to government minister. By contrast, women work mostly in the subsistence or "informal" sectors. In Latin American cities, four in ten women workers are domestic servants — notoriously low-paid and with very poor and unstable working conditions — while a number of the others are street vendors or have casual jobs. As a result, women's earnings are typically far lower than men's and they enjoy almost no benefits like medical coverage or pensions.

Even when women gain access to good jobs, they are often paid much less than men for the same work. The ILO reports that women's pay scales are ordinarily 75 percent of men's, and in some countries — like South Korea — as low as 50 percent. Women work far more often part-time and their unemployment rate is substantially higher as well.

Women in every country face expectations and social pressures that keep them in the home, away from the world of wage work. In North Africa and the Middle East, where many urban families consider wage work for women to be dishonourable, women make up only 13 percent of the formal labour force. Patriarchal culture, favouring "modesty" and household work, rules in nearly every region — machismo in Latin America, purdah in many South Asian countries. Religious traditions frequently lend their authority to these practices.

Even women who gain formal wage-based employment rarely work as many years as men. Most take time off to raise children or care for family members and they are pushed out of the labour force at an earlier age than men. By law, many countries require women to retire at an earlier age than men — usually five years earlier. So women have far less opportunities for job advancement, they accumulate less personal savings, and they have far fewer pension benefits. A 1987 survey of elderly in Chinese cities found that the proportion of women with no income was eleven times higher than the proportion of men. This is because many women did not work long enough in a state enterprise to become eligible for pensions.

Some observers argue that "development" actually harms the majority of women in later life rather than benefits them. Cut off from subsistence, often lacking support from kin, without stable employment or pension, they face conditions that are arguably worse than what they enjoyed in traditional village society.

Official statistics show that very few women "work" after the age of 60 — only one in a hundred in Jordan, typically about 10 percent in other countries of the South. But employment statistics, biased towards wage work, tend to ignore many kinds of women's productive activity, especially in later life. In reality older women work very hard for their own sustenance and the welfare of other family members, mostly in "informal" work, outside the wage sector. They work many more hours than older men and often at more physically exhausting tasks, such as agricultural labour in family fields, carrying water or gathering firewood. One study in a Nepalese village found that older women work 11 hours a day — about half in productive work such as agriculture and half in household labour. By contrast, older Nepalese men, with practically no household tasks, work only half as much as the women. In Africa, where women do almost all of the agricultural work, the gap between men's and women's labour can be even greater.

ILO, prodded by women researchers, has tried to develop statistics more inclusive of unpaid work, more reflective of women's contribution and older women's constructive engagement. The goal is laudatory, but few countries have shown much interest. Only work that results in market exchange interests the economists, government planners and business managers. "Granny labour", however essential, remains invisible.

To obtain income, some older women work outside the home more intensely than ever before in their lives — often as market vendors, producers and sellers of street foods, laundresses, seamstresses and so on. African women are especially active later in life as processors and sellers of meat, fish, fruit and other foodstuffs. In Nigeria, older women do a great deal of fishing. In India, many work as domestic servants. At a time of life when men are helped by pensions, property rents or support from younger wives, older women mostly depend on their own labour to meet their essential needs.

Ironically, though women's income needs are especially urgent, international self-help organizations have not seen the importance of gender targetting. A 1991 study of 150 projects found that only one — a project to support the purchase and raising of cows — had specifically aimed at older women.

Under the old patriarchal culture of past centuries, women suffered discrimination as objects of men's power and desire. But in many countries today, "development" has not brought a decline in the objectification of women or a greater appreciation for the beauty of later life. Quite the contrary. The culture of industrial capitalism, with its cosmetics industry, barrage of erotic advertising, and youthful movie and television stars, defines feminine beauty more than ever as the sole province of youth.

Freedom from sexual objectification in later life may bring a hidden compensation for some women, though. In some cultures, women after menopause gain greater freedom to enjoy public life than in their earlier years. In parts of the Caribbean, Latin America, the Middle East and Africa, women sometimes emerge in later life as strong figures in their community, able for the first time to travel, to make new friends and to engage in business. Reports from Lebanon, Jamaica and Ghana confirm this, serving as an inspiring reminder of women's potential strength and capacity in later life and their need for freedom from sexually-defined subservience.

Divorce and widowhood

Some women may be liberated by the departure of a spouse, but many find only disadvantage as husbands die, or divorce or abandon them. In middle-age, the overwhelming majority of women are married (or live in equivalent partnerships). Typically, they are married to older men — an average of two years older in China, five years older in India, and ten years older in Senegal. Since women live longer than men, and are married to older men, their husbands will probably die first — six or seven years earlier at least. Women, then, are likely to spend much of their later life as widows. Amazingly, among all people over 60 in the South, men and women combined, nearly half are widows. Generally they are the poorest and those most seriously at risk.

Older married women also face the prospect of divorce or abandonment — both thought to be on the increase worldwide. In casual or "visiting" marriages, not uncommon in the Caribbean, relationships typically dissolve and men drift away. But even in ordinary marriages, men can terminate the relationship, under some traditional customs and laws, and they usually assume no responsibility towards their former spouse. The older woman, unlikely ever to remarry, may be suddenly cut off from her social world, including often her children and grandchildren. Dispossessed of family land, denied access to those she loves, deprived of housing, and shorn of social status and belonging, the divorced or abandoned woman may return to live with her kin. As kinship support dissolves, she is highly at risk in later life.

Older men who are widowed or divorced remarry more often than older women. Many cultures frown on women's remarriage and put barriers in their way, especially in the higher social classes. In India, remarriage among upper-class Hindu women was absolutely forbidden. Some Indian women practised *sati*, burning themselves alive on their husband's funeral pyre; from the state of Rajasthan, there have been recent reports of women being forced to submit themselves to this hideous ritual. In the past, Hindu widows had to shave their head, wear special clothes, eat a restricted diet and give up most social contacts. These harsh customs, though no longer followed rigorously, still influence a good many women. Economic necessity, though, often leads to remarriage among working-class women. A widows remarriage act and government campaigns have promoted second unions as well.

China had a traditional ban against remarriage of widows, and in the upper classes of Korea the ban was so stern that even if a bridegroom died before the marriage ceremony, the "widow" was expected to remain "faithful" and never "remarry". In South Korea, the government eased legal barriers to remarriage only as recently as 1960.

Women usually find it difficult to get remarried. Rules of mourning and modesty everywhere put barriers in the way of widows. Strict social sanctions on sexuality and friendships with men make it hard for them to have contact with future partners. Since most men remarry, the problem is rooted more in demography than in social custom. There just aren't enough men to go round. In Tunisia, among men of 65-74, fewer than one in ten are widowers, whereas among women of the same age more than half are widows. In Indonesia, for the same age group, about one in ten men are widowers but seven in ten women are widows. Five or seven women for each single man in later life and the odds are getting worse!

No wonder, then, that arrangements of older women living together are on the rise, sometimes even with government encouragement. China has rural living arrangements for widows without family support by which three women live together in a government-supplied house. Hong Kong and Korea encourage sharing of two-person urban apartments for the elderly as well. Given the scarcity and expense of single-person living quarters, this trend is sure to continue.

When a husband dies, widows in some cultures maintain their authority within the family. But in many lands, they lose their previous prestige and social status. A widow who lives with children and grandchildren may lose authority in the household in favour of her daughter or daughter-in-law, especially if she loses ownership and control of the family home and farm. Family members may now view her as a bother or a burden, or treat her as a servant. For the great majority of poor widows, conditions continue to decline even as old patriarchal customs fade. In most Southern countries, and especially in the cities, increasing numbers live alone and with no family support, fending for themselves.

Inheritance and pensions

Patriarchal legal systems compound the problems of older women, especially widows. Both law and legal-cultural traditions restrict women's ability to own property, as well as their access to civil court and their rights to divorce. Older widows often cannot inherit property, such as the house, small business or farm they shared with their husband.

Legal reforms in recent decades have not always succeeded in putting women on an equal footing with men. Nor have new laws changed stubborn patriarchal customs. In India, legal changes such as the Hindu succession act of 1955 improved women's formal inheritance claims, especially in the absence of a will. But men began to use wills to exclude their wives from an inheritance. And the cultural tradition that women could only inherit *moveable* property — furniture or clothing, as opposed to a house or farm — proved stronger than the new law. Even today, a woman who wants to claim her full legal property rights after the death of her husband must win the cooperation of others in the family — people who may have a strong interest in getting the inheritance themselves. To maintain good family relations, most women never try.[2]

Polygamy and patriarchal religious traditions make matters worse. A woman in Niger complains:

> I was the first of three wives... When you live alone with your husband, sharing of land poses no problems because it all goes to your children. It is more complicated when there are children by other wives. Then, if the father dies, the land is divided between everyone. According to Islam, the man has a right to twice the woman's share.[3]

From the early 1900s onward, most official reforms liberalized marriage and inheritance laws. Turkey changed its laws in the 1920s from Islamic to a secular basis, while South Korea and Brazil introduced reforms favouring women in the early 1950s. Everywhere, though, customs continued to resist women's claims. Since about 1980, religious-based political movements have reversed reforms, especially in Islamic countries, where governments have revived *sharia* laws which enforce women's legal inequality.

Recent land-reform laws, though not influenced by Islamic doctrine, have reduced traditional women's rights to the family farm after the death of their husbands. New laws in Kenya and Tanzania ignored women's rights completely and established exclusive male ownership. These and many other inheritance laws pass a husband's property directly to the male children of the marriage, bypassing the wife more or less completely. If a woman is childless, or if she has only female children, the husband's property may pass to other family heirs, such as the husband's brothers. All too often, the heirs force the widow to move out of a family home, to give up use of a family plot of land, and to turn over animals, vehicles, tools and other vital necessities — the basis of the widow's life and livelihood.

Pension laws often don't protect widows either. Some give widows half or less of their late husband's pension benefit, creating a sudden and devastating decrease in their incomes. More recent systems and those primarily based on individual contributions are often no improvement.

Health, disabilities and care-givers

Women are far more likely than men to be sick and disabled in old age and their expectancy of life *without disablement* is shorter than men's. The reasons may be partly biological, but the greatest cause is likely to be different life patterns and opportunities. The Pan American Health Organization thinks there are four main social influences. First, throughout life, women have less access to food. Second, women bear the health burden of many births. Third, women suffer from greater life-long poverty and discrimination. And fourth, they are worn out by the double responsibility of work and domestic chores. Air pollution from cooking fires is a further factor which probably causes later-life illness and disability. Women are just beginning to speak out on the terrible burden of physical abuse they suffer from husbands and male kin, abuse which often has a long-term effect on their health.[4]

Older women suffer disproportionately from a host of disabling conditions, like osteoporosis, diabetes, blindness, and arthritis, as well as depression. A Latin American author, referring to the life of the majority of women in Brazil, describes them as "physically and spiritually old before the age of 30".[5]

Though women do most of the care-giving, they lack care-givers for themselves, especially in later life. Children, who used to take care of frail family members, are now in school, and daughters or other younger women are now often away at work. Older women take care of their husbands, but their husbands rarely take care of them. In Ghana, for instance, more than half of all older men report that when they are sick, their wives take care of them. But only 4 percent of older Ghanaian women report that their husbands provide care when *they* are sick. Similar patterns have emerged in Latin America and Asia. Some of the difference can be explained by the fact that men die first. But husbands who are alive do not as a rule see caring as their responsibility either. So older women depend on a mélange of different (usually female) care-givers: daughter or daughter-in-law, sister, grandchild, niece, neighbour and friend.

Older women have less access to health-care services than older men, according to women's health advocates. The main reasons are women's modesty, their greater distrust of health-care institutions, lack of money to pay user fees, and their lower level of health insurance coverage. Older women also often testify that they face prejudice from medical personnel.

Migration, war and epidemics like AIDS weigh especially heavily on older women. As children move away or die, they leave grandchildren behind, with no one but grandma to look after them. More and more grandmothers are assuming this "skip-generation" role, an unprecedented level of responsibility and an unbearable demand on the grandmother's slim resources. In some parts of rural Africa, as many as a third of all older women have children or other dependents, including even a few "old-old" parents.

Reforms that target older women have been few and far between. The 200 million elderly women in the countries of the South are not only the most vulnerable but also the most invisible people on the planet, from the point of view of international policy planners and aid-givers. Even women's rights advocates often forget the special needs of their older sisters, as the great international conference in Nairobi (1985) bore witness.

Efforts to improve conditions for older women must begin by improving the condition of women at earlier ages. Better education, nutrition, maternal health and job opportunities for girls and young-to-middle-age women will contribute significantly to women's chances later in life and improve their later health substantially as well. The global women's rights movement seems to be making progress in these areas. Women's education, in particular, has improved dramatically in recent years.

Legal reforms, new efforts to ensure equal rights of inheritance and further progress in the social and legal aspects of divorce and widowhood are also urgently needed.

Above all, the deep poverty of older women must be addressed head-on. Some will propose more welfare measures, like food-aid, widow's income support, subsidized housing, subsidized medicines and the like — "poverty-reduction" World Bank-style. Such welfare measures are likely to be refused by governments, and in any case are far from ideal. The only stable and long-term solution to poverty is access to appropriate work, at decent pay, for all those older women who are fit and ready for employment. Self-help projects must be targetted directly at women, and rural development schemes must recognize the needs and rights of older women.

NOTES

[1] Adapted from a case study described by Nana Abt at an expert group meeting on the integration of ageing and elderly women into development, UN Office on Ageing, Vienna, Oct. 1991.

[2] On this, see Pramila Dandvate, *Widows, Abandoned and Destitute Women in India*, New Delhi, Radiant, 1989, p.4; and Jaya Sarma Gujral, "Widowhood in India", *Widows*, Durham, 1987, Vol. I, p.47.

[3] Nigel Cross and Rhiannon Barker, eds, *At the Desert's Edge: Oral Histories from the Sahel*, London, Panos, 1992, p.129.

[4] To those who think that women's condition improves with "development", women in India have pointed out that the number of cases of husbands who have burned their wives to death ("dowry deaths") have increased sharply in the 1980s and that the largest number is in the capital city of Delhi.

[5] Coelho de Faria, as quoted in Sheila M. Peace, *An International Perspective on the Status of Older Women*, Washington, International Federation on Ageing, 1981, p.39.

8. Housing, Care and Social Life

"If an old age home were built in Morocco, I believe it would mean the country no longer existed," quipped King Hassan II a few years ago. "Moreover," he continued, "I would be the first to burn it, in an act of auto-da-fé."[1] Like Hassan, many leaders in the South express strong opposition to institutional care and housing for the elderly, claiming to speak in defence of local customs, national culture and the family system. But increasingly, such sentiments seem out of touch with reality. In Casablanca, not too far from Hassan's royal palace, old people sleep in the streets, abandoned by their families, or forced out of their homes by rising rents.

On every continent, unprecedented homelessness confronts the elderly. Elder homelessness plagues Hong Kong as much as Kinshasa, Bangkok as much as Accra.

In the villages older people often live in pitiful smoke-filled hovels, with leaking roofs, damp dirt floors and little light or air. They lack the money or physical capacity to maintain their home, much less improve it. As they grow older and as migration carries away their younger kin, their homes frequently fall into disrepair and decay. In the cities they crowd into small airless apartments with many other family members, or live alone in a tiny room or barrack bunk; toilets and running water are luxuries that few can afford. As city after city falls prey to feverish real-estate speculation, glamorous office buildings and luxury residential towers rise in former low-rent neighbourhoods. And older people lose their homes.

Booming Hong Kong, at the cutting edge of market modernization in Asia, offers a glimpse of where other countries may be heading. There, grandparents can't find enough space to live with their children and grandchildren because developers have torn down old residential buildings where apartments were large enough to accommodate three-generation families. And the public housing authority has built new apartments so small they cannot accommodate both younger families and elderly parents.

Unscrupulous landlords, particularly in poor, overcrowded neighbourhoods like Mongkok, take advantage of Hong Kong's desperate elderly. Some offer "cage homes" — triple-high bunks, enclosed in lockable wire cages, dozens of which are crammed into large rooms of old buildings. More than a thousand elderly men live in these cages, paying rents as high as US$70 a month. Other elderly live in rooftop shanties or tiny cubicles barely large enough for a bed.

Religious groups were the first to respond to Hong Kong's housing crisis, by providing shelter alternatives to the elderly in the mid-1960s. By the late 1970s, Christian churches had set up 22 homes and hostels, many located within public housing estates and benefitting from government subsidies. Finally, as the numbers of Hong Kong elderly soared in the 1980s, the government began to talk about improved public housing arrangements. But the rules, which give priority to large families, continue to discriminate against small households of older people. Sixty thousand are on housing waiting lists for one- and two-person units, with waits of at least five years and often as much as ten.

In the 1980s, Brazil and Botswana, worried about declining family support for the elderly, took steps to reverse the decline of three-generation housing. They built some bigger apartments to accommodate all family members and gave housing preference to large households that included grandparents. Another new housing programme promoted near-by living, with small units for older people alongside larger units for their children and grandchildren. Some governments began to allow — and even encourage — unrelated older people to live together.

Most reforms bogged down in economic hard times. As governments slashed their budgets, they rarely gave priority to elderly housing. Budget reductions at the local level also trimmed or eliminated housing programmes of provinces, cities and townships.

In China, housing for the elderly emerged as a crisis in the early 1990s. Nearly one in six rural elderly lack shelter with their kin and many have lived in special homes supported by work units or regional governments. According to some figures, by the mid-1980s there were 27,000 such homes, known as "rural elderly shelters", or "houses of respect", housing at least 280,000 people. Today's market-based changes have stripped away resources from these homes; the communes, now defunct, used to fund them, and local governments have not taken over full responsibility. Their future is in doubt, just as China's elderly population is soaring.

In China's cities, public enterprises own and run millions of housing units for retired people and "social welfare community centres" serve as homes for the poor elderly who have no other housing options. But subsidized housing may soon disappear. World Bank-sponsored reforms are pressing the Chinese government to eliminate low-rent enterprise-based housing. Already, enterprises are selling developers their old-style *hu tong* housing, with low-rise buildings built around a central courtyard. These structures are located in central cities, on land which now has high redevelopment value. Mrs Wu is one such elderly victim of these changes. Aged 70 and living on a small pension, she resided in central Shanghai in an old enterprise-owned building. In 1992, she was informed that the building would be torn down, and she was offered a new apartment on the outer fringe of the city, far from her friends, from shopping and other amenities.

As dwellings are privatized, rents will almost certainly rise rapidly, making housing unaffordable to many elderly. Chinese commentators admit that resources are now shifting towards market-based, high-cost privately-run homes for rich older people. While newly-rich older Chinese enjoy comfortable accommodations, elder home-lessness, rare in China for over forty years, is certain to spread rapidly.

Old age "homes" are the most controversial type of housing for the elderly. Some provide just a residence, with food and recreation in common, while others (often called "nursing homes") provide health care for the chron-ically ill. A few such homes are wonderful and welcoming places. More often, homes are frightful prison-like institu-tions, closely regulated and with little privacy.

In Mauritius, a number of older people are housed in the same facility as the disabled and the mentally ill. Government homes in Trinidad are broken down, under-staffed and so poor they cannot even afford to buy essential food and clothing for their indigent residents. People look on these homes as a fearful symbol of poverty in old age.

Catholic charities and municipalities in Latin America built many homes throughout the continent, especially for the poor. In the mid-1980s, Mexico had 150 homes, Ecuador 30. The great majority of the homes are dilapi-dated, vermin-infested, filthy and depressing, a kind of "cemetery" of the living, as one author put it. A report on Ecuador's homes speaks of inhabitants "vegetating and waiting for death".

Governments often requisition unused old buildings for the sites of homes. With grim symbolism, they com-monly take over chronic disease hospitals, military bar-racks, convents, even prisons. Crumbling structures con-tinue to decay, while within, neglect of patients is the rule, not the exception. People often live in dormitory-style rooms, with virtually no privacy. In Argentina, 32 residents of a government-run home died of malnutrition in July of 1990; afterwards, a government minister re-signed in disgrace, but two years later she was appointed head of PAMI, the country's largest social programme for the elderly![2]

A report from Chile concludes that among the poor residents of homes, most "resent their solitude, their institutionalization" and they "feel abandoned by their own families and friends in particular and by society in general".[3] Inactive and depressed, many do not even develop friendships with other residents, living withdrawn and bitter lives.

In spite of doubts about the value of the homes, their numbers are growing nearly everywhere. In Taiwan, nearly one in twenty people over 65 was living in a home by the mid-1980s. In Israel and Singapore, the proportion was closer to one in forty, in Costa Rica and Hong Kong, one in fifty. Some governments are promoting homes as a substitute for families, which are increasingly unable to take care of their elderly.

In a few countries, government reforms have improved lives in homes for the elderly. But very poor conditions remain the rule. As authorities cut health-care and public-service budgets, the funds for homes have often been the first to get the axe.

Meantime, though, homes don't seem to be running out of customers. Families and public authorities may force some older people to enter, but other elderly clearly make the choice on their own. Ken Tout tells of a home set up in an abandoned Latin American prison, with just 13 nuns taking care of 750 sick inmates. Tout was astonished to see a waiting list of several hundred applicants. For many desperate, homeless elderly, life in a home, with regular food and shelter, was "much preferable to hunting scraps on the rubbish dumps in the streets outside".[4]

Deepening poverty and declining family support have forced many countries to consider expanding long-term care for their poor elderly, even when policies opposed such institutions. In Egypt where the government had closed several homes in favour of family-based care, authorities reluctantly opened new facilities in the late 1980s. In Kenya, the government has quietly provided subsidies to several dozen private old age homes. The Kenyan type of partnership between government and religious or citizen organizations grew rapidly in the 1980s, especially in Africa.

African institutions for the aged are typically small and very simple. Zimbabwe's 81 homes have an average of fewer than twenty residents each. Most lack health-care facilities and government support, and residents or community people must often secure the food supplies and do the cooking and other housework. Scarce resources do not always lead to worse results, as two homes in Zimbabwe illustrate.

The Kudzai old people's home is a church-supported home with relatively nice facilities, including indoor toilets and baths, beds, a dining hall and a well-equipped clinic. By contrast, Dumbudzo old people's cooperative has outdoor toilets and baths, mattresses without beds and no dining hall; it has twice as many occupants per room as Kudzai. But the residents of Dumbudzo are far more satisfied with their life. By contrast with Kudzai, where a paid staff runs the home and takes care of the residents, the residents at Dumbudzo are actively involved in every aspect of the home: they grow grain, raise animals, cook and serve the food and participate in money-making schemes like weaving mats. Apparently, Dumbudzo residents enjoy their participation, self-reliance and social cooperation; work is a means for them to continue a full meaningful life.

Melfort old people's cooperative in Zimbabwe was founded in 1979 by a nun using similar principles of self-help. Its forty-odd residents — both men and women — support themselves by farming, raising corn, tomatoes, beans, groundnuts and cucumbers, as well as rabbits and chickens. They cook, clean and run the home and they even bury their own dead. In years with good rainfall they have enough surplus to buy themselves clothes, bicycles or other commodities.[5]

Another such home in Kenya, established by the Presbyterian Church in 1967 in a Kikuyu village, is perhaps one of the earliest cooperative homes. The home houses fewer than twenty people, all of them destitute and without family, on a very small budget supported by the church's women's guild. A single staff member comes six days a week to cook and work in the garden. The residents themselves do all the rest of the work — and much of the gardening.[6]

As economic changes bring tens of millions into the cities every year, people of every age face a deepening housing crisis. In most cities, market forces are not producing adequate shelter and governments are pulling out of public-sector housing development. In that context, older people are likely to suffer especially, with their very low income and their special housing and care needs. Cooperatives, care in the home and other innovations may soften the blows of this harsh period, but only deeper reforms affecting work and income are likely to change the fundamentals of the elderly housing calamity.

Entertainment, education, social life and home care

Older people suffer from depression and physical decline when they stay at home with nothing to do. So governments, churches and other citizen groups have organized clubs, entertainment, social events and educational institutions to keep the elderly socially engaged. Increasingly, these elder clubs emphasize sports and physical exercise, too. And some are organized directly by the elderly themselves.

Most governments, however neglectful, have some new services they can claim to their credit. South Korea (which has virtually no pensions) has developed 4000 *noinjong* throughout the country. In these "pavilions for the aged", older people socialize, play musical instruments and enjoy games. Singapore has built an "ageing village" — a kind of Disneyland of ageing — on the outskirts of the city, providing recreation and education, addressing physical and mental health issues, and offering advice on the transition from employment to retirement.

China has built by far the largest programme to promote the social life of the elderly. The government-sponsored National Committee on Ageing has encouraged local citizens to set up associations of the elderly in thousands of neighbourhoods and villages. The associations may organize social services or it may represent the needs of the elderly to local governments. The national committee has set up sports associations and educational institutions as well.

Mexico set up a national programme in 1980 under the auspices of the National Institute on Ageing, providing day centres as well as social services. Mexico also has a programme known as the Council of Elders, a federal agency for the rural and urban poor. The Cuban government set up *casas de los abuelos* (grandparents' houses) in the 1980s — community centres for day care of older citizens, with staff, kitchen, common rooms, patio and garden. By 1992 there were 43 of these centres serving 3400 people with health care, meals and social services. Coverage was far wider with the *círculos de abuelos* (clubs of grandparents), set up in 1986, which grew by 1992 to 7500 clubs with 165,000 members. The clubs organize outings and cultural events and they have been active in a campaign against sedentariness, running exercise classes. Early in the morning, all across the country, older citizens assemble in local parks and public squares and on beaches to go through a series of gentle aerobic exercises, just as they do in China.[7]

The government of Costa Rica set up the Costa Rican Gerontological Association in 1980 as its arm for elder programmes. It has been at work promoting senior centres by working with local communities. It supports programmes in yoga, music, theatre and dance, promotes coverage of ageing issues in the mass media, and develops exercise and sports activities including an annual seniors' road race.[8]

With support from UNESCO, China pioneered in developing "universities of the third age", now a world-wide movement. The term "university" is a misnomer. Rather, these are adult-education programmes, often run and taught on a volunteer basis by retired school teachers, offering courses in health, nutrition, horticulture, physical exercise, art and the like. Such programmes in China and elsewhere are at once innovative and conservative. Learning has been very empowering for many illiterate elders, who have never attended school. Literacy courses offer the most positive part of the curriculum and have led to far more engagement of older people in local political and social issues. But predictably, officials see the universities not as a route to empowerment and liberation but as a means to get the elderly to "adapt" to their forced inactivity and to channel their energies into harmless pastimes.

In some countries, the main drive to organize programmes for the elderly has come from private organizations rather than governments. Religious institutions have often been among the first to set up elder clubs and "daycare" facilities. The Hong Kong Council of Social Service coordinates the work of many service agencies, including the Hong Kong Christian Service, which runs a senior citizens' service centre and a health promotion project. In Singapore, church and citizen organizations have taken the lead in providing social activities for older people. The Salvation Army and the Red Cross have been active there and ethnic clan organizations in particular have set up neighbourhood facilities and organized social events.

Everywhere, programmes are including elderly members in planning and doing work. In the Mexican city of Cuernavaca, a group of local professionals helped set up a neighbourhood centre of this type. A regular paid staff helps run the centre, but the fifty elderly members are deeply involved in its operation and management. They help tend a vegetable garden, cook meals, wash dishes, and have an important voice in most decisions. They also help distribute food to those who are too sick or disabled to come. Daily life at the centre includes physical exercise, parties, dancing, discussions and courses on personal care and health.[9]

Another related organization in Cuernavaca reaches out to older people in market-places, churches and clinics. It, too, is based on organization and leadership by the elderly themselves. A third elderly-run project offers free legal services based in an accessible stall in the city market-place.

On the Caribbean island of Dominica, destitute homebound elderly are so numerous that a special organization called REACH has been formed to serve them. REACH workers first must find these older people, who usually live alone, in tumbledown shacks, often sick, mentally confused, incontinent and malnourished.

The HelpAge network of organizations has helped set up caring organizations and day-care centres in a number of countries. Funding from the parent organization helps cover the costs of the premises and a regular staffperson. The elders who use the facility provide much of the labour and make most of the decisions about operations and programming. HelpAge also encourages self-help work projects to supplement the income of those the centre serves.

Informal groups sometimes provide critical psychological and social support for older people, too. Older men get together in bars, coffee houses, town squares or public parks to meet with friends, play cards, or participate in less strenuous sports like lawn bowling. Women get together in more private ways, but they form support groups, too. In Turkey, strong women's networks come together in one anothers' homes, helping widows stay connected to friends and warding off the loneliness of later life.

As programmes and support systems for the elderly multiply, their humane and caring purposes should not obscure the possibility of deeper and more effective solutions. They contribute only very partially to overcoming the enforced idleness, poverty and loneliness of unemployed elders. Exercise programmes, dances, study courses and outings may bring joy into some lives, but for most elders, they can be no substitute for work, bread, housing and primary health care.

NOTES

[1] As quoted in Jeannine Jacquemin, "Elderly Women and the Family", *Soroptimist International*, n.d., p.1.

[2] *El Pais*, 27 February 1994. The minister of health, later head of PAMI, was Matilde Svatetz de Menendez; she insisted she was not responsible for the starvation incident.

[3] Carmen Barros et al, *La Vejez Marginada*, Santiago, Magdalena Aguirre, 1979, pp.25-26.

[4] Ken Tout, *Ageing in Developing Countries*, New York, Oxford University Press, 1989, p.140.

[5] Andrew C. Nyanguru, "Residential Care for the Destitute Elderly", *Journal of Cross-Cultural Gerontology*, vol. II, 1987, pp.345-57; "The Melfort Old People's Co-operative of Zimbabwe", in Tout, ed., *Elderly Care: A World Perspective*, pp.47-52.

[6] Maria G. Cattell, "Caring for the Elderly in Sub-Saharan Africa", *Ageing International*, June 1993, p.18.

[7] See Robert Dacal, "Alternatives to Institutions: Various Options for Support of the Elderly in Cuba", in Tout, *Elderly Care*, pp. 53-59.

[8] Zaaida Esquivel, "Programmes of the Costa Rican Gerontological Association", in Tout, *ibid.*, pp. 106-11.

[9] Celia Ruiz, "Organizing Older People in a Mexican Community", *Ageing International*, March 1993, pp.17-18.

9. The Ageing Movement

The ageing movement and the United Nations

Eva Peron, wife of the Argentine president, came to New York to address the UN general assembly in 1948. With charm and passion, she offered the delegates a universal declaration of old-age rights. Her proposal affirmed older people's right to food, clothing, health-care and work, as well as to assistance, recreation and respect, and recommended UN studies to implement elder rights in the name of "the fuller social and economic protection of mankind". Coming not long after the landmark Beveridge report in Britain, and only months after the Universal Declaration of Human Rights, the time seemed ripe for international action on the rights of the elderly.

UN delegates adopted Eva Peron's proposal — but only as a draft. Many governments had their doubts about elder rights. In an effort to bury the document, ambassadors insisted that the Universal Declaration itself provided adequate protection. Voting on the resolution was postponed indefinitely. But advocates of special rights for the elderly continued their efforts. In 1950, secretary-general Trygve Lie raised the issue himself, in a report to the UN social commission entitled "Welfare of the Aged: Old Age Rights". Again, governments blocked the call to action. The secretary-general's report was soon forgotten. Eva Peron's draft declaration stayed on the agenda for twenty years, ignored. Then it, too, was scrapped.

Governments preferred to avoid broad humanitarian commitments, choosing to work instead on limited and more flexible goals like pension improvements. They did this within the framework of ILO. In 1952, at a major ILO conference, governments agreed to broaden pensions and social security and to set "minimum standards" for pension coverage in old age. Positive as these steps were in some respects, they had relatively little impact on conditions in the South, where many countries had yet to emerge from colonialism and pension systems were rare.

On other issues, like minorities, refugees, women and the disabled, governments eventually agreed to international conventions and new institutions. Children attracted great concern, and UNICEF became their champion. But governments put old age on the back burner and steadily blocked any special international mechanisms to protect or empower the elderly.

In the 1950s, 1960s and 1970s, as governments dragged their feet, citizen groups arose in many places to defend and promote the rights of the elderly. In the United States, citizens founded two major ageing organizations in the 1950s, and in Europe organizations like England's Help the Aged emerged at this time as well. In the South, most organizations started just a short time later — Indians founded Senior Citizens' Clubs in 1970 and the Association of Retired Persons of India in 1972. Kenya, Sierra Leone, Pakistan, Colombia, Argentina and many other countries saw new organizations come to life as well. The International Federation on Ageing, set up in 1973, helped knit together this worldwide movement, which continued to gain momentum in the 1980s.

As concern grew, writers produced important books on ageing, professors turned their attention to the new field, scholarly journals appeared, and population studies began to show that the world's population was "ageing" faster than anyone had expected. Global ageing as a field of enquiry emerged, a hybrid of anthropology, sociology and economics. In the 1960s, Nana Abt started her pioneering studies of ageing in Ghana.

Studies highlighted the emerging crisis. From every region of the South came alarming reports that older people suffered unemployment, poverty and abandonment. At a 1968 conference organized under UN auspices, social welfare ministers took up the issue of ageing with a new sense of urgency. The following year, the government of Malta proposed a UN general assembly agenda item on "the question of the elderly and the aged". No declaration of rights was proposed. Again, governments preferred to ignore the issue.

A few countries of the South, searching for solutions, took initiatives of their own, especially more urbanized countries and those with more government revenue. Venezuela set up the *Patronato Nacional de Ancianos y Inválidos* in the 1960s and began to build old-age homes. Nigeria held a government conference on ageing in 1974. Brazil and Mexico took steps about the same time to broaden their pension systems.

In the North as well as the South, ageing issues gained visibility and public backing. By 1977, the general assembly discussed the question of calling a major international gathering on ageing under UN auspices. The following year, on 14 December, delegates voted to convene a global assembly on ageing in 1982

> as a forum to launch an international action programme aimed at guaranteeing economic and social security to older persons, as well as opportunities to contribute to national development.

To prepare for the assembly, the UN organized regional preparatory meetings and asked countries to present information about their national programmes. In 1981, the general assembly designated an annual "Day for the Ageing". Drafting went forward on a "plan of action", to be put before the world assembly delegates. Regional meetings took place in Malta, Costa Rica, Bangkok, Lagos, Washington and Bonn. In the flurry of interest and activity, many countries created planning and research projects as well as permanent ageing institutions. Mexico set up the *Instituto Nacional de la Senectud* (national institute of old age) in 1980; Nigeria hosted a conference of African experts in 1981; China set up a vast National Committee on Ageing in 1982.

From 26 July to 6 August 1982, over 1100 delegates from 124 countries converged on Vienna to attend the world assembly. At a symbolic level, the assembly was a victory for all those who had fought for the international rights of the elderly, affirming the importance of older people's lives and envisioning their future as full participants in the world community. But it proved disappointing in terms of concrete achievements.

In the preparatory sessions, even before the delegates gathered, governments had signalled their opposition to major initiatives and (above all) major new budget outlays. Assembly draft documents affirmed the need to *reduce* public spending for income security, medical care and social services, because of deepening economic troubles.

In the assembly itself, speakers often mentioned the consequences of a new austerity. Leticia Shahani, UN assistant secretary-general for social development and humanitarian affairs, referred in an opening address to the deepening worldwide recession that had already imperilled economic and social programmes. Coming cutbacks in social services, she admitted, would adversely affect a large number of the elderly. Delegate after delegate pointed to the ravages of unemployment and inflation, insisting that governments could do little for the elderly in the face of decreasing resources. Family care, traditions of respect and voluntary organizations figured often in discussions as alternatives to government programmes.

On the critical issue of employment, advocates for older persons argued that improved health and longer lives meant retirement should be postponed, age limits removed from labour legislation and full employment rights expanded. But many governments demurred, stressing the problem of youth unemployment and the preference of employers for younger workers. The European countries in particular, coping with rising unemployment, stood firmly against broadened employment rights in later life.

Some had hoped that a new UNICEF-like agency — provisionally called the United Nations Fund for the Aged (UNIFA) — might emerge from the assembly. Again governments balked, worried about the added budgetary costs and the policy directions that might emerge from such an institution.

The world assembly's great achievement was an ambitious 62-point plan of action, to set targets, to guide government planning and to provide a framework for monitoring progress in the years ahead. Less than a statement of rights, the plan of action was still much stronger than any existing international document. The plan contained some striking and quite dramatic language, including the affirmation that conditions of the elderly in the South can only improve in a different and more just international economic order and the expectation that fundamental new policies will probably only arise as a result of political pressure brought to bear by rising numbers of older people. Governments were called on to "facilitate the participation of older persons in the economic life of the society".

The assembly gave rise to a sense of accomplishment if not euphoria. But the follow-up eventually deflated expectations. The new UN Ageing Unit, based in Vienna and intended as a "focal point" for all UN action on ageing, received only modest funding and a limited mandate. Its small professional staff, led in the early years by the able Tarek Shuman, could not possibly answer the tremendous global needs for information and advocacy. They did succeed, though, in giving ageing a new level of visibility in the UN system, and they carried out two very useful international progress reports on member states' work within the plan of action. The UN Population Fund gave a major boost to ageing work when it took up the issue in 1984 and began to fund much of the major research, as well as conferences, training and information exchanges. In spite of these efforts, UN programmes continued to address the elderly all too often as objects of humanitarian assistance, rather than as actors in the process of social and economic development.

Governments themselves were slow to put in place machinery for ageing policy. National committees on ageing existed in only 29 out of over 120 countries of the South according to a UN survey in late 1987. Of these, only 14 had representatives of organizations of and for the elderly.

Thanks to an initiative by the government of Malta, the UN set up an International Institute on Ageing at Valletta — a centre for training professionals from countries of the South. WHO expanded its own work on ageing and health. Here and there, in international conferences and institutions, ageing advocates established a presence. And governments grew increasingly aware that something had to be done.

The indefatigable Julia de Alvarez, UN ambassador from the Dominican Republic and distinguished leader on ageing issues within the international diplomatic corps, pressed on with her long campaign to establish a statement on elderly rights. To emphasize the productive dimension, she added "responsibilities" as well as rights, but few delegates were ready to agree.

Disappointed by opposition, she called on the International Federation on Ageing in 1989 and worked with IFA leader Charlotte Nusberg for the next two years to draft a rights statement with input from elderly organizations worldwide. Alvarez and IFA representatives took the finished text, with its enormous global backing, to the ECOSOC Commission on Social Development in early 1991, hoping at last to get action. But the West European countries, led by Germany, put up an unexpectedly fierce opposition. As always, the core of resistance centred on the concept of older people's "right to work".

Alvarez and her allies eventually accepted a compromise: the statement expressed "principles" rather than "rights", and references to work were amended to remove the critical statement on age discrimination: "no barriers based on age". In the autumn of 1991, the general assembly adopted the statement of principles. Like the plan of action, it was a symbolic advance, but disappointingly short on potential for action.

As the tenth anniversary of the World Assembly neared, the UN Ageing Unit assembled nine international experts in the spring of 1992 to set new global "targets" for the aged for the year 2001. In the prevailing climate, the targets remained modest and relatively uncontroversial. The anniversary passed in the autumn of 1992, with but one new initiative. Thanks to Alvarez's prodding, the assembly designated 1999 International Year of Ageing.

After nearly fifty years, international action under the UN leaves much still undone. The general assembly, the World Assembly and the Ageing Unit have made many positive statements and now ensure that ageing is not forgotten. The UN Population Fund and the UN university have sponsored very useful research studies. But many countries, including the richest and most powerful, have blocked more ambitious projects. And the destructive actions of the World Bank and the International Monetary Fund — themselves UN-related and (in theory, at least) subject to control by the general assembly — have undercut the well-being of older citizens worldwide.

Advocates of elderly rights continue their efforts at the UN and in other global gatherings, convinced that solutions to the problems of ageing can emerge only through international cooperation. Country delegations, especially from the South, are now speaking more often about the need for global action on elderly issues. A very active

NGO committee, in partnership with major international ageing groups and a group of sympathetic experts, has been raising ageing issues more frequently in international gatherings like the International Conference on Population and Development and the World Summit for Social Development. Slowly, alliances are being built between ageing advocates and others, like women's rights groups and advocates of children. But major progress still awaits a mobilized community of elders worldwide.

Organizations of the elderly

Experts on ageing like to talk about "empowerment", but they usually mean a chance to make simple choices — like a voice in deciding a community centre lunch menu or a say in running a self-help bakery. Important as this kind of power may be, it has no leverage over the big issues like employment, health care and income security. Empowerment, as is often pointed out, has a paternalistic ring; it assumes that older people cannot take control of their own lives, that someone else must give them the right to self-determination, that they are capable of only very limited kinds of social action.

Some analysts insist that older people cannot be politically effective because of declining energy, lack of enthusiasm and the tendency to be easily discouraged.[1] All too often, gerontologists, doctors, social workers and welfare bureaucrats claim to speak in the name of older people. Church leaders do the same.

But reality confounds the experts' paternalism. Thousands of large and active seniors' organizations have sprung up in several countries in the past fifteen years, including some — like ProVida in Latin America or SoCO in Asia — with sponsorship, help and inspiration from religious bodies. They prove that power and dignity can be won through the activity of older people themselves and that far more is at stake than lunch menus.

In practically every country of the world, active and powerful elder organizations now exist as well as networks of senior centres as a base for political action. Among the national groups are the Singapore Action Group of Elders, the Pakistan Senior Citizens' Association, the Indian Federation on Ageing, Korea Senior Citizens' Association, China National Committee on Ageing, National Council of Senior Citizens' Organizations of Malaysia, HelpAge Kenya, Association of Pensioners and Retired Workers (Tanzania), ProVida Bolivia, the *Movimiento Unificador National de Jubilados* in Mexico and the *Movimento pro Idosos* in Brazil, to name just a few.

In many countries, three or four national organizations, as well as dozens of specialized agencies and institutions, give voice to the needs and concerns of older citizens. India has four major national organizations — two that speak for pensioners, as well as the Federation on Ageing and HelpAge India.

Governments have founded some of these organizations and use funding and direct appointment of leaders to limit their independence. In countries where governments insist on conformity, even a term like "empowerment" can seem too radical, according to a retired military officer who is founder of the Pakistan Senior Citizens' Association. Too many ageing organizations are still run by government insiders; they dispense patronage and provide window-dressing for official policies on ageing. Others uncritically accept government sponsorship, like the majority of Singapore's 166 older people's clubs. But major elder organizations, under pressure from their members, are casting off their previous subservience and new groups are challenging the status quo. Like it or not, governments have to confront demands for elderly rights and tolerate (or even support) what they might have previously seen as subversive. The government of Uruguay set up a centre for information, promotion and action on the rights of the elderly in 1993 — to give information and legal advice that is sometimes used against the government itself.

More and more, independent groups of elderly organize to confront governments and to engage in direct action in the national political arena. During Argentina's pension crisis, militant elder groups came to the fore, including a new elder-based political party, the *Partito Blanco*.Similar parties have been founded in Chile and Peru.

In some countries, elder groups have formed powerful coalitions, embracing trade unions, women's groups, religious bodies, and student movements. A growing understanding that *everyone* will grow old some day, that everyone has a stake in elder issues, promises more coalitions in the future. In Colombia, women's groups took a leading role in the campaign for social security which began in 1986, demanding expanded pension and health coverage for women, especially women domestic workers.

Argentina shattered traditional myths about passive old people during a militant grassroots campaign against the 1992 pension cuts. The movement started spontaneously in the senior centres of Buenos Aires, as older people formed half a dozen different protest groups. Uniting their efforts, they borrowed a tactic from the women's human rights movement that brought down the military dictatorship. Beginning in April 1992, they held a round-the-clock vigil in the Plaza de Mayo, enduring great cold and hardship until they were finally expelled by the police in early June. After that, they began a vigil and protest every Thursday in the plaza outside the headquarters of the national parliament.

Several hundred elderly participated each week. Sometimes they held sombre marches, their leaders carrying the national flag. Occasionally, they stopped traffic, occupied government buildings, and even scuffled with police and government officials in the streets of the capital.

On many occasions, protesters were arrested, but sometimes armed riot police withdrew before them, unable to frighten and unwilling to club down these dignified grandmothers. On 2 March 1994, thousands of elderly converged on the centre of the capital to mark "a hundred weeks" of these dramatic protests.

Sixty-two-year-old Norma Pla, who founded a group called "Jubilados de Plaza de la Valle", has been the movement's most prominent leader. A favourite of the media, she fascinates because of her strong personality and her fiery determination. Neither a member of a traditional political party, nor a person ever before in the spotlight, she has proved naturally charismatic, with a few missing teeth, a gift of eloquence, and a sure political sense of timing.

The Argentine government tried to discredit the movement by accusing it of being infiltrated by "troublemakers" and bankrolled by sinister enemies of the ruling party. But the feisty elders had attracted too much public sympathy. Feeling the heat, the government agreed to make some concessions. It raised pensions for the oldest old. It agreed to pay some of the money owed to destitute pensioners (especially the oldest old) in cash, and it promised a future reform of the pension system. The government did not restore the old pensions, though. So protests continue.

The biggest victory of the Argentine elderly is not to be measured in pension money but in their increased self-respect, independence and self-empowerment. They will continue to make their voices heard, there can be no doubt. Few would have imagined they could accomplish so much in such a short time.

Halfway around the globe, in a very different culture, elderly Chinese have been organizing in Hong Kong, under the leadership of the Society for Community Organization (SoCO), founded by Christian social activists in 1972.

In the late 1980s SoCO launched a campaign to organize neighbourhood elders in mutual aid committees. The committees started with a half-dozen local activists, then expanded rapidly through local meetings and personal networks of friends and neighbours. Resourceful and energetic elderly members have organized health clinics, consumer coops, educational groups and benevolent societies. They also have helped their neighbours obtain rights — to free telephone service, dental care and medical treatment.

As the committees gathered momentum, they began to address larger political issues. They have carried out surveys, designed by members, to expose problems in the neighbourhood and in the city more generally. Their housing surveys were an embarrassment to the government, exposing as they did bad conditions in public housing, as well as the plight of the cage people and the homeless, and revealing the gap between official rhetoric and the reality of people's daily lives.

Similar efforts of elder organizing are going forward in many other countries. In the face of terrible life conditions and outrageous prejudice, older people are embarking on a life-affirming struggle that may change human existence in the years ahead. Slowly, they are forcing younger people to realize that they, too, will be older one day.

The church and the elderly
This book had its origin at a consultation organized by the World Council of Churches to consider the church's ministry with senior citizens. That ministry has a

long history, and finds expression in a variety of programmes.

Churches run elder hostels and old-age homes, social services such as home care and meals-on-wheels, senior centres, and a number of special programmes that address particular social problems in the lives of older people. Many of these have been eminently successful, and some have pioneered in specific areas. In recent years local churches in many parts of the world have sponsored workshops, cooperatives, job banks and other projects for older people to find paid and volunteer work in their communities.

We need to consider carefully whether our programmes meet the criteria of self-determination and dignity the elder movement has been setting. We must ask: are older people involved in the decision-making processes; does the programme foster self-reliance and the integration of older people in family and community; does it give them a sense of worth and pride; does it, in short, enhance their life or is its main thrust only to prepare them for death?

In all their work, churches must shake off age-discrimination — looking upon older persons as frail and sick and as objects of care and charity. More old-age homes and hospitals for the chronically sick will not meet the needs of the new era. Instead, we must make every effort to include the elderly as full participants, putting an end to ghettoized old people's programmes.

Churches do some of their best work on a small, local scale, where their roots are deepest, but they should not content themselves with such efforts alone on behalf of older people. Rather, they should join coalitions with other religious and secular groups to press for the broad rights of older people — at the UN, in the financial institutions and aid agencies, and in national parliaments. They should also use their moral authority to speak through the mass media — newspapers, magazines, television and radio — on behalf of elder rights.

Churches can promote more dialogue and cooperation between the generations — particularly between older people and youth — by developing special programmes for this purpose and by considering the special contribution to the faith community of people in each phase of the life-cycle.

Churches must of course give special attention to the spiritual issues and priorities of the new conditions of long-life. People in their later years tend to reflect back on their lives, trying to make sense of all they have experienced. This process can and should include the support and affirmation of a community of faith. Older people also need the assurance that a caring community can bring, especially when they face bereavement and other unanticipated, difficult changes in their situation.

But churches need to attend to the body as well as the soul; they must join in the struggle to develop, strengthen and protect pensions and other income-support programmes, as essential security for all people, especially those who are frail or sick. Arguments that such support payments are "too expensive" must be totally rejected, as long as ostentation, waste, corruption and warfare appropriate large shares of the world's social wealth.

At the same time, health-care, prevention and wellness strategies must be adapted to the needs of the majority of older people, not just elite hospital patients. This means that the entire health system and its professional priorities need to be reviewed, and recast in favour of programmes that promote and strengthen wellness rather than patch up the sick. Far more should be done to create caring health institutions that are responsive not only to physical conditions but also to human beings with individual personalities, life circumstances and values. Churches, with their commitment to the spiritual dimension of life, are well-placed to bring this emphasis to health services.

As a "message to the church" issued by the WCC consultation said, the church is "the covenant community of faith where life is affirmed and transformed". On the basis of that affirmation the message called upon the church "to develop an educational framework for living and ageing", "to be a conscience, voice, monitor and advocate, as it relates to the ministry and role of older adults", "to train and to retrain older adults to participate in a changing world", and "to create an environment in which intergenerational sharing and ministry can occur".

Yet another message from the Pakenham consultation said:

> Ageing is a global reality which touches each of us on a personal and community level. Ministry involves the act of covenanting and making the promise to commit one's life, gifts and talents for the welfare of the community. Ministry with senior citizens is formed in a community and covenant context. The church's ministry is not a patronizing act, but rather a call to work with our brothers and sisters who are aged. We are interdependently linked in the life-affirming process of ageing. As the way of Christ we participate in the ageing process. We become stewards who are called to bring justice in relationships, promote peace, and affirm the integrity of creation, further enhancing the future of our planet and the next generation.

By learning more about the needs and gifts of the world's elderly, by affirming the full dignity of persons in later life, the churches will discover more completely their own calling.

NOTE

[1] On older people and political action see Henry Pratt, "The Emergence of Seniors Organizations: An International Perspective, *Ageing International*, March 1993, pp.9-11; S.M. Zaki, "Senior Citizens Unite", in Ken Tout, ed., *Elderly Care*, p.94.

Short Bibliography

Nana Abt, *Aging in Ghana*, Legon, University of Ghana, 2nd ed., 1985.

F.S. Braithwaite, *The Elderly in Barbados*, Barbados, Caribbean Research & Publications, 1985.

Ai Ju Chen and Gavin Jones, *Ageing in ASEAN: Its Socio-economic Consequences*, Singapore, Institute of Southeast Asian Studies, 1989.

Giovanni Cornia, Richard Jolly and Frances Stewart, *Adjustment with a Human Face*, Oxford, Clarendon, 1987.

Doris Davis-Friedman, *Long Lives: Chinese Elderly and the Communist Revolution*, Stanford, Stanford University Press, 1991.

Mary Jo Gibson, *Older Women around the World*, Washington, IFA and AARP, 1985.

Irene Hoskins, ed., *Older Women as Beneficiaries of and Contributors to Development: International Perspectives*, Washington, AARP, 1992.

Hal Kendig, Akiko Hashimoto and Larry Coppard, eds, *Family Support for the Elderly: The International Experience*, New York, Oxford University Press, 1992.

Kevin Kinsella, *An Aging World II*, Washington, Bureau of the Census, 1993.

Helena Z. Lopata, ed., *Widows*, Durham, North Carolina, Duke University Press, 1987.

William McGreevy, *Social Security in Latin America*, Washington, World Bank, 1990.

David R. Phillips, ed., *Ageing in East and South-East Asia*, London, Edward Arnold, 1992.

Kasstury Sen, *Ageing: Debates on Demographic Transition and Social Policy*, London, Zed Press, 1994.

Lee Sennot-Miller, *Midlife and Older Women in Latin America and the Caribbean: A Status Report*, Washington, AARP & PAHO, 1989.

Tarek Shuman, ed., *International Conference on Population Aging*, San Diego, University Center on Aging, 1993.

Ken Tout, *Ageing in Developing Countries*, New York, Oxford University Press, 1989.

Ken Tout, *Elderly Care: A World Perspective*, Andover, UK, Chapman & Hall, 1993.

United Nations, *Ageing and Urbanization*, New York, UN, 1989.

United Nations, *Economic and Social Implications of Population Ageing*, New York, UN, 1988.

United Nations, *The World Ageing Situation: Strategies and Prospects*, New York, UN, 1985.

United Nations, *The World Ageing Situation 1991*, New York, UN, 1991.

John B. Williamson and Fred B. Pempel, *Old Age Security in Comparative Perspective*, New York, Oxford University Press, 1993.

World Health Organization, *Ageing in the Western Pacific: A Four-country Study*, Manila, WHO, 1986.